Motivation

Powerful Motivators That Will Turbo-Charge Your Workforce

Also by Paul Levesque

Customer Service Made Easy

Motivation
Powerful Motivators That Will Turbo-Charge Your Workforce

Paul Levesque
Illustrations by the author

Entrepreneur®
Press

Editorial Director: Jere Calmes
Cover Design: Perlman Creative Group
Editorial and Production Services: CWL Publishing Enterprises, Inc., Madison, Wisconsin, www.cwlpub.com

This is a CWL Publishing Enterprises book developed for Entrepreneur Press by CWL Publishing Enterprises, Inc., Madison, Wisconsin.

This publication is designed to provide accurate and authoritative information in regard to the subject matter covered. It is sold with the understanding that the publisher is not engaged in rendering legal, accounting, or other professional services. If legal advice or other expert assistance is required, the services of a competent professional person should be sought.

> —From a Declaration of Principles jointly adopted by
> a Committee of the American Bar Association and
> a Committee of Publishers and Associations

ISBN 13: 978-1-59918-141-7
      10: 1-59918-141-x

Library of Congress Cataloging-in-Publication Data

Levesque, Paul, 1947-
    Motivation : powerful motivators that will turbo-charge your workforce / by Paul Levesque.
        p. cm.
    Includes index.
    ISBN 978-1-59918-141-7 (alk. paper)
    1. Employee motivation. 2. Motivation (Psychology) 3. Organizational change. 4. Organizational effectiveness. I. Title. II. Title: Powerful motivators that will turbo-charge your workforce.
    HF5549.5.M63L465 2007
    658.3'14—dc22

                                                    2007033494

Printed in Canada.

11 10 09 08 07   10 9 8 7 6 5 4 3 2 1

Dedicated with love to my brother John Levesque
and sister-in-law Renee, who prove that
"close family" and "close friends"
need not be mutually exclusive terms

Contents

Introduction

On his second day in the house he'd rented, Len was finding the place a bit chilly. He located the fancy temperature control panel but couldn't understand any of the buttons and switches and flashing lights. He did, however, spot the word HEAT under two buttons shaped like up and down arrows. He pressed the up-button, and was pleased to immediately hear the furnace in the basement roar to life. That should take care of it, he thought.

What he couldn't hear, moments later, was the outdoor air conditioning system activating automatically. Programmed to maintain a constant temperature in all the rooms, it poured cool air into the house.

By day three Len was growing weary of always feeling cold. He pressed the up-button several times to pump more heat into the place. Unknown to him, the air conditioner automatically intensified its own output in response.

For the remainder of the month Len had the furnace going full blast day and night. He remained unaware that the air conditioner, too, was operating at full capacity around the clock.

"So, how do you like the house?" the owner asked on the last day of the month.

"I'm not renewing my lease," Len said. "The furnace is useless. Plus, the energy bill in this place is insane."

This is what attempts to motivate employees can often feel like. Most such efforts don't work—or don't last. No matter how hard managers try to raise the motivational temperature of their employees, it seems, things always seem to slide right back to the chilly, who-cares climate that is the norm in most workplaces.

What's everyone doing wrong?

The problem often stems not so much from what businesses are doing, but rather from what they're *un*doing. Even among those that do succeed in raising employee morale every now and again, the improvement is typically short-lived. Elements of their organizational culture keep turning motivation right back into cynicism, enthusiasm right back into apathy.

Look at the literature. Virtually all books and articles on this topic list ways to activate various heating factors (motivators), while offering very little, if anything, on how to deactivate the biggest cultural cooling factors (demotivators). This glaring oversight—both in the literature and in common practice—helps explain why so few efforts to motivate workers have any positive lasting effect. The huge cumulative investment businesses make in warming up their organizational climate is undone by the cooling factors built right into their basic cultures.

Motivated About What?

If a married couple were to tell friends they're investing a lot of time and effort in an attempt to make their children more "eager," the first question out of the friends' mouths would be, "Eager about what?" When these friends learn the parents have no specific answer and are just seeking to make their children more eager in some vague "overall" sort of way, they might be inclined to see this is as a poorly defined objective with little chance of success.

The examples that fill most books on motivation represent efforts to get workers more motivated in precisely this kind of vague "overall" sort of way. These books treat employee motivation as the objective in and of itself, with little or no consideration given to what the employees should be motivated *about*.

In reality, demotivation, low morale, apathy, cynicism—these and other related conditions are all symptoms of a single larger cultural ailment. They're the inevitable indicators of a business that's not collectively "on a mission," not driven by a shared sense of purpose, not aligned in pursuit of an exciting primary goal everyone can believe in and get behind. In such a business, there's nothing that *moves* workers to give their all, which is precisely what "motive" means in its most basic dictionary sense—a word related to motion, a word to describe something that moves people to act in some particular way. The business has not given its workers a motive to leave their comfy beds in the morning and actually *look forward* to the work day ahead. The employees have no motive to resolve their differences and find ways to work together in order to achieve an objective everyone considers equally important and worthwhile. They have no motive to give any more of themselves on the job than the very minimum required. As you read these words, thousands upon thousands of workers in every kind of organization across the country are doing as little real work as they can safely get away with. There's nothing moving them to do more.

The existing literature provides an endless laundry list of "500 ways to motivate your workers," or "2,000 techniques for boosting employee morale." The very fact that such "heating factors" are listed in the hundreds or even thousands may hint at how long their effect is expected to last in the deep-freeze climate of businesses operating without motive.

This Book vs. All the Others

In these pages you'll find a strategy for turning off the major cooling factors *and* turning up a variety of heating factors *at the same time*. The chapters to come spell out how to make one single primary business objective the basis for a fundamental "culture shift." As we'll see, this alignment of the culture along a single, clear mission everyone can get excited about is what gives workers their motive. It not only turns apathy into enthusiasm, it also creates an environment that *maintains* the enthusiasm over the longer term. Instead of "3,600 Ways to Motivate Your Employees for a Very Very Short Time," this is "The One Sure-Fire Way to Motivate Your Employees for Keeps."

Another way in which this book differs from the others—virtually all of them confuse "incentive" with "motive" and treat the two terms as completely interchangeable. Webster's New Universal Unabridged Dictionary (1996) emphasizes the distinction: "MOTIVE is applied mainly to an inner urge that moves or prompts a person to action," whereas "INCENTIVE ... is today applied only to something offered as a reward." Inner urge *vs.* outer reward—that's a pretty significant difference. Despite the word "motivate" in their titles, most other books instead offer up example after example of employee incentives, in answer to the unspoken question that (it has long been assumed) is forever at the back of every worker's mind: *What's in It for Me?* The book in your hands focuses primarily on motive, rather than incentive. If there really is an unspoken question at the backs of most employees' minds, this book assumes the question to be more along the lines of *Why Should I Care?* This is a book on giving workers a reason to care.

One final major differentiator for the book in your hands. The others list incentives (prizes, tokens, gifts, bonuses, "gold stars" of every description) that are all forms of *internal* recognition, expressions of appreciation that originate from managers inside the organization. This is the equivalent of children receiving reward and encouragement from caring parents inside the home. While such feedback is obviously essential for the child's well-being on a number of levels, its motivational impact diminishes quickly. Many children sooner or later find themselves wondering, "Are you just saying these nice things because you're my parents?" It's not until the child begins receiving *external* recognition—expressions of encouragement and appreciation from impartial teachers, coaches, and judges from outside the home—that the motivational effect really becomes significant and lasting.

Workers, too, after receiving a succession of plaques and prizes and other tokens of appreciation from management, can begin to wonder just how legitimate and sincere all this internal recognition really is. Could it all be part of a manipulative attempt to keep employees doing things the way management wants them done? It's not until employees begin receiving expressions of approval and encouragement from impartial sources *outside* the organization—from suppliers, and partners, and especially from customers—that the real motivational effect kicks in.

One of the recurring themes in this book is the pursuit of continuous positive feedback from delighted customers. This is the kind of external recognition that has the greatest (and most enduring) motivational impact on employees, and it's at the very heart of the strategy outlined in these pages.

The traditional management preoccupation—if not obsession—with the bottom line has always left most workers cold. The traditional countermeasure, repeated attempts to heat things up by throwing cash and incentives at employees, has produced spotty and short-lived results. If it is the organization's cultural focus that is ultimately sapping workers of their motive to give their best efforts, then any serious attempt to restore motive will necessarily mean changing the cultural focus.

This is a book that spells out a surprisingly simple process for shifting your own organization's cultural focus. It's almost impossible to win at anything unless you have a motive to do so—and there's nothing more motivating than consistently winning. This is the guiding principle behind the book: a manual on how to provide your employees with a powerful motive to win, and on how to use their wins to keep them motivated.

Acknowledgements

Even in organizations crackling with energy and excitement, the principles and mechanisms that govern employee motivation tend to operate behind the scenes and can therefore seem mystifying until you have an opportunity to peer behind the curtain and study what's going on at close range. It's been my happy privilege to be allowed to poke around in a wide variety of such organizations, and I owe a great deal to all of them.

Many individuals in such businesses were generous enough to submit to lengthy interviews for this book, for which I am extremely grateful. They include Lynne McLaughlin and Sharon Holdcraft of Dunkin' Donuts (along with several members of their staff, and even a few customers); author and consultant Cheryl Beall of Retail 101; Beth Guastella of Kate Spade stores; Mark Emmitte of Stage Stores; Brain Gallagher of Lindt & Sprüngli; and Paula Davis at General Motors. Further insights were provided by my friends Peter Ambrozaitis and Cathi Rittelmann at Novations Group.

Thanks to my lifelong buddy Andy Parisien, and to my brother-in-law Brian Simpson, for the willingness you both had to wear an appropriate mask when the situation called for it. You know what I'm talking about. And a huge thank-you to Yvon Douran at Keynote Resource, for all your generous help and support.

This is my second book for Entrepreneur Press, and once again Jere Calmes and the whole EP team have made the experience a pleasure from the very beginning. A special nod of appreciation to Karen Thomas, whose capacity to exceed expectations seems limitless; to Stephanie Singer for her always-cheerful collaborative spirit; and to John Woods at CWL Publishing for his unfailing willingness to go the extra mile.

This is ultimately a book about creating cultural alignment within organizations. I wanted to find a business that could serve as an example of such alignment—that is, a business in which all the various elements that shape and define organizational culture have been pulled together as part of a single successful initiative or program. With the help of my wife Sandra, I found a superb example of this kind of alignment in Delaware North Companies' *GuestPath* program. I therefore owe a huge debt of gratitude to DNC's Stewart Collins, who very generously provided an unrestricted close-up view of the program's inner workings. Thanks as well to DNC's Camille Maxwell for additional background, and to Sandra Levesque, who first brought the program to my attention. At the time of this writing Sandra is one of the newest additions to the company's senior management team.

Sandra also happens to be the great love of my life, a post she's held for over a dozen years, now. Anyone who remains unconvinced about the contagious nature of enthusiasm and motivation need only spend a short time with my beautiful wife to experience it for themselves. Anyone lucky enough to spend day after day with her over a period of years will become such an expert on motivation, he could write a book about it.

Chapter 1

Making Work Feel Like Play

"**I** don't pay my workers to have a good time. I pay them to get the job done."

Chances are this statement summarizes the philosophy of at least one boss you've had over the course of your own work career. It is, after all, an *extremely* common managerial point of view. "Employees are hired to work, not to play. There's a huge difference between the two." (There certainly is—a difference every bit as great as the one between faltering businesses and thriving businesses, as we'll soon be exploring in more depth.)

Question: if in the past you've had bosses who held this view, were they the ones who drew the very best work out of you? Were they the ones who inspired you to willingly go the extra mile for them and for the company? In short, was this when you personally felt most motivated on the job?

I was about 10 when one day I saw my granddad working hard with a handsaw to trim the end of a plank of wood and asked what he was doing. He paused to take out his handkerchief and mop his brow, saying, "This piece of wood is giving me a lot of trouble. I've cut the end off it twice now,

1

and it's *still* too short." For a 10-year-old, this unexpected collision with absurdity—delivered with such seemingly stone-faced conviction—was enough to make both knees weak with laughter. In the years since then, however, I've encountered many situations where the same kind of absurdity was being pursued with *genuine* conviction, and have tended to find it much less hilarious. Trying to put out an actual fire with kerosene isn't all that comical. Trying to cure obesity-related health problems with diet schemes that "allow" all kinds of high-calorie treats doesn't lead to particularly amusing results. And in businesses crippled by employee demotivation, there's nothing very funny about trying to correct the problem by adopting a get-tough stance that only makes things worse. The old gag "FIRINGS WILL CONTINUE UNTIL MORALE IMPROVES" is always good for a laugh—until we recognize that it's describing, without all that much exaggeration, an actual approach to employee motivation that continues to affect the lives of real people in a great many real organizations.

So let's talk about work and play over coffee and a donut.

The Busiest Donut Store, and Why

There are some 6,000 Dunkin' Donuts stores in 30 countries, with over 4,400 stores in the U.S. at the time of this writing. Of course only one of these outlets can qualify as the "busiest" in the entire chain. For quite a few years that distinction has belonged to a store located about 11 miles southeast of Boston, on Route 18 in South Weymouth, Massachusetts.

This one outlet earns more than $3 million a year, serving between 2,000 and 3,000 cups of coffee per day. The store is owned by "George's girls," the three daughters of the late George Mandell, who bought it in 1974 and quickly turned it into an extremely successful operation. Today there are some 65 employees on the payroll.

A quick tour of the premises uncovers a number of features that set this store apart. For example, there are two separate drive-thru lanes—a regular one, and one marked *Express*, which does not offer all of the options available in the *Full Serve* lane.

"The drive-thru really is a store within itself," says co-owner Lynne

Mclaughlin.[1] Her sister Sharon Holdcraft explains that the workers in the drive-thru part of the store operate as a fully self-contained unit. "They have all of their own equipment, they don't share any equipment with the front of the store, so pretty much everything they need to service their customers is right there. We have two of everything."[2] "It makes it a lot easier for the employees, they're not bumping into each other," Lynne adds. "They usually have four people with headsets on, just working this area. It's its own little business."[3]

"Look at the drive-thru," laughs long-time regular customer James B. Gallimore. "It's constant, if you ever notice. It's constant."[4] It's hard *not* to notice the unending stream of vehicles moving continually past the store's large windows.

Another difference in this store—the products are baked on-site. "Not that [the product in other outlets] isn't fresh and up to standards," says Lynne. "It is. But it's still not coming from the back room to the shelf."[5] Customer Gallimore is asked why he and his wife Dorothy drive across town virtually every day to stop in this store, despite the fact that there's another outlet much closer to where they live. "They make their donuts

here," he says, "and the other places, they have them delivered, and that makes a big difference."[6]

The Gallimores are typical of a great many of the store's regular customers who return daily for reasons that may also have as much to do with a sense of community as with a love of the product. "Coming in here so often," says Dave Marden, a regular for many years, "you get to meet a lot of the people that are here, and I even run into friends from long ago here, frequently."[7] Sitting across from Dave is Ed MacEachern, another long-time regular. "A lot of friends come here," Ed agrees, "like Dave, some friends, we sit down...."[8]

The customers also cite another of the store's key attractions—its employees.

Dave Marden sums up the staff with one word: "Excellent."[9] Ed MacEachern agrees: "They're very personable, they try to wait on you right away."[10] "They are friendly," offers Dorothy Gallimore. "You know what it is? [At most places you] don't get service today. I mean, you go in a supermarket, you're just a number. It's sad. Here they make you feel like you're family."[11]

When co-owner Lynne is speaking about the store, her remarks are often cut off in mid-sentence to allow her to call out greetings to various customers, often by name. She's asked what proportion of the store's clientele represents repeat business and quickly surveys the population of customers in the store at that moment. "Look around," she laughs, speaking as much to her sister as to her questioner. "They're *all* regulars!"[12]

Another appealing feature of this store: "You don't wait a long time in line," in Dorothy Gallimore's words.[13] Many of the other customers' comments similarly emphasize the speed of the service they receive. "This goes back to my father's philosophy on how to run the store," co-owner Sharon explains. "You use your business tools, and if [the volume of business suggests] you should have one-and-a-half staff members, well, ninety-nine percent of franchisees would just go to one—and he would go to two."[14]

"*Perception*," says Lynne emphatically. "People come in, there isn't a huge line, so [they think], 'All right, I have time to stop, it won't take too long."[15] "Even if it looks busy," Sharon says, "they'll be willing to stop because they know they're going to get through pretty much as quickly as they would have otherwise. Really it's just that it's all moving so quick, 'cause there's enough people behind the counter to work it."[16]

The Roots of Motivation

There are no "employee motivation" programs in this organization, so where does all this collective energy and shared determination-to-succeed come from? Tracy Brown, 31, has been on staff for four years at the time of this writing. She works in the small out-building from which Express drive-thru customers are served. Must be pretty boring work, in pretty cramped quarters, right? "*No*," she blurts without hesitation, "I *like* it! The time goes by fast, because I deal with millions and millions of customers every day. I like working with people. I have regular customers that come in every single day, and they're happy and they say hi to me, they know my name, you know, so I like seeing them every single day, that's what makes me happy. If one of my customers isn't there that day I'm like, 'Hey where were *you*?' the next day. So that's just what I like. I like working with people."[17]

Another employee, 21-year-old Amy McCaul, works up front in the main part of the store. Does her job ever become a bit boring? "No way. It's a good environment to work in—it's fun, it's busy, time goes by fast, you're always doing something."[18]

Completely independently, both workers mention time passing quickly. This may seem an odd coincidence, until you discover as I have over the years that virtually *all* motivated employees say the same about their work. In a documentary video I produced with Andy Parisien in 1995, for example, a young employee at one of Canada's most successful fast-food restaurants told me, "I'm having an amazing time. I work, and I don't realize the time. And I'm happy."[19]

Losing track of time is of course the very *opposite* of the traditional "clock-watcher" image of an employee bored stiff—and it gives us an early clue about the nature of employee motivation. In his landmark 1990 book *Flow: The Psychology of Optimal Experience*, Mihaly Csikszentmihalyi (former chairman of the Department of Psychology at the University of Chicago) describes what he calls "The Transformation of Time":

> One of the most common descriptions of optimal experience is that time no longer seems to pass the way it ordinarily does.... Often hours seem to pass by in minutes; in general, most people report that time seems to pass much faster.[20]

The psychology professor is summarizing a study that explored what enjoyable human activities actually feel like. Most people associate this kind of enjoyment with a favorite hobby or game or pastime, and only very seldom experience anything like it while on the job earning a living. Yet workers in business settings that are aligned and energized clearly often experience, as a routine part of their work lives, the kind of enjoyment usually associated with play activities.

Amy McCaul describes her job in a donut store as "fun." Asked if she occasionally receives good comments from customers, she replies, "All the time! It makes you feel good because it feels like you actually have an impact on how their day goes. You think back to those moments, and you would miss that customer if they didn't come back. But those are our regular customers that say that to us—and then there's customers that come in from, you know, another state, and they're like, 'Wow, this place is *awesome*, I've never been to a Dunkin' Donuts like this, you're all so friendly, and it's very fast service, and it's the *best*.'"[21]

Tracy Brown offers an example: "A lady came through, and she's like,

'You guys are so great, I come all the way from down the other end of Weymouth to come here because you guys are quick, and you make my coffee the best. And she actually said it, and I was like, 'Oh thank you.' It made me feel good, because she traveled to come to my Dunkin' Donuts."22

To "my" Dunkin' Donuts—does this employee have a strong personal identification with her work? Here's another hint: when asked if one day she might like to own a business similar to the one she presently works for, her boisterous reply is, "Yes, I would like this one!"23

There is *something* in this workplace—and in the many other similarly energized work settings I've visited and studied over the years—that makes the work so enjoyable for employees, they describe it in terms most people reserve for their favorite play activities.

And in other business settings, even those where the employee demotivation problem is severe, individual workers will often participate in recreational activities away from work—activities they find *highly* motivating. We begin to understand the true nature of employee motivation when we more fully understand *human* motivation as it relates to play.

Why Do Bowlers Bowl?

Though work and play are very different animals, the actual kinds of activities that make up both can sometimes be surprisingly similar. Both can involve periods of extreme physical exertion, for example, along with periods of total inactivity. Both can represent a series of tasks repeated again and again, often with seemingly little or nothing to show for the effort beyond the knowledge that it was accomplished. What, then, are the specific elements that make play feel so much more engaging than work for most people?

I could use any game or sport or other leisure activity to illustrate the principles involved, but I'll use bowling because it's an activity even most nondevotees are reasonably familiar with.

Without intending to offend anyone, let's begin by acknowledging that bowling (as is also true with golf, or dart-throwing, or any other similar activity you can name) is *in and of itself* a pretty pointless exercise. Knocking

the same objects down over and over again, in exactly the same way—only to have some contraption undo your achievement and set the objects right back up again exactly as they were before you knocked them down—would seem a sure-fire recipe for an infuriating experience. But not only do avid bowlers not find this assignment boring, repetitive, and pointless, they often can't wait to get at it. It helps them forget the boring, repetitive, and pointless jobs that earn them enough to pay for the pleasure of bowling.

There are four basic elements that make bowling (and other play activities) fun and motivating. The absence of these same elements in most work settings is why most workers hate their jobs.

1. An Element of Challenge or Difficulty

"Bet you can't hit that tree over there with a rock."

It's an absolute must—to be enjoyable, a game *must* be difficult to win. It must require certain skills or talents that not everyone has. Young children understand this perfectly. When they invent games for each other, there's almost always an element of challenge involved: "Bet I can outrace you to the store."

If the main source of satisfaction in darts is to score a bull's-eye, wouldn't the game become a lot more satisfying if players stood much closer to the boards, and the bull's-eyes were larger? And in golf, why complicate things with clubs and long fairways—why not just walk directly over to the hole with a bucket of balls and drop them in by hand, one after another? Big savings in time and money.

Children's games like paddle-ball, leapfrog, skip rope, and others are often based on a "keep the kettle boiling" theme. A sequence of separate actions is defined, and then the challenge becomes to see who can perform the sequence most quickly and most often without making a mistake. Speed is a key element in games of this type. Speed is also a key element in energized businesses like our donut store, where employees seem to be perpetually moving in fast-motion, where customers consistently remark on the speediness of the service. The owners design the layout so that workers are not bumping into each other. This is "keep the lines moving through the store," "keep the cars flowing through the drive-thru," "keep the shelves stocked with fresh product," "keep the customers happy and coming back." The whole operation is one big keep-the-kettle-boiling game from opening time to closing time, and the workers love the challenge. Ask them why they have so much fun on the job, and they tell you how they love being kept busy, love how time goes by fast, love dealing with "millions and millions of customers every day."

Compare this with more conventional work settings, where managers are often reluctant to entrust workers with a mission that "might be too challenging for them." The only big challenge for workers in these kinds of places is how to stay awake—or perhaps how to resist the urge to head home and never come back.

2. A Clear Set of Rules, Understood by All

"We each get 10 tries to hit the tree with a rock, and we have to stay behind this line when we're throwing. Whoever hits it most times wins. Loser pays for the ice cream."

In play activities, all players understand what the one primary objective is, and what they are and aren't permitted to do to achieve it. The rules are simple, straightforward, easy to remember. Everybody knows what a perfect score would look like.

If new players are joining the game, someone will outline the objective and the rules for them. It's always a good sign if the new players break into a hint of a smile as the rules are being explained—it means they're thinking, "This is going to be fun." If the new players' expressions turn more toward frowns or scowls, this is not such a good sign. It could mean the objective is confusing, or the rules seem too convoluted and difficult to remember. If the explanation of the rules goes on and on forever, the new players may decide whadya know, they no longer feel very much like playing after all.

As we'll see in Chapter 3, a business that's aligned is by definition a business driven by one single primary objective that everyone understands, and that takes precedence over all other considerations. An example of such an objective might be "Do whatever it takes to keep customers happy and coming back." More common is the work setting in which there is no one single overarching objective, but instead a host of very different—and even conflicting—priorities that leave workers unclear from moment to moment about where they should be directing their main efforts and energies. Combine this with unclear rules in terms of organizational values or guiding principles, or rules and regulations that never end, and workers may decide whadya know, they no longer feel very much like working after all.

3. A Scoring Mechanism to Provide Immediate Feedback

"So far you've hit the tree twice, and I've hit it four times—that's four-two for me."

Play activities are set up so that the players know how well they and everyone else are doing at all times. Especially in competitive contests, this is what keeps things challenging. It's the primary source of pressure, of incentive to try harder—of motivation, pure and simple. And even in non-competitive activities (such as playing "catch," for example), the participants will still often be inclined to track their performance in some vaguely score-related way: "That's the fifth catch I dropped. Last time I only dropped two. I must be slipping."

Remove the mechanism for clear and immediate feedback, and the enjoyment level for that particular activity drops like a stone.

LEISURE

"Bowling In The Dark" Meets With Resistance

Hiding pins in darkness takes all the fun out of the game, bowlers say.

By Al Bishop
Associated Times

The controversial practice of hiding bowling pins in darkness, so bowlers can't see them while playing, is meeting with increasing resistance from bowling groups across the country.

"We were hoping people would see it as a way to add a fresh new element of suspense to the game," says National Bowling Federation chairman Merle M. Tisdale. But it's not working, according to Dallas broadcaster Ernie "Buzz" Braddox, host of the weekly TV show *Bowling For Dallas*. "The minute you take away the satisfaction of seeing those pins go

believe it's having the opposite effect.

"All you can do now," according to Madelaine Lefebvre, 42, " is let the ball go and watch it disappear into the darkness, and listen for an encouraging sound. Then some weeks later your scores arrive in the mail. Where's the fun in that?"

Bowling In The Dark began in 1999, when a blown electrical circuit at an alley in Atlanta plunged the pins into darkness. Bowlers kept playing, and the manager saw a way to cut expenses. Before long word spread to other alleys.

"I installed special light shields in all three of my locations," says Luke Coggins of Bowlerama. "That cost money. Now it looks like I'll have to pull everything out and go back to standard lighting. How am

ASSOCIATED TIMES SYNDICATE

Bowlers in Fort Lauderdale cope with being unable to see the pins as they play. Many who have tried it complain that waiting to receive their score in the mail robs the game of all enjoyment.

In energized business settings such as our donut shop, the immediate feedback comes in the form of appreciative comments from happy customers, the generous tips, the "millions and millions of customers" that continue to show up all day long, day after day. Their work earns these employees a steady stream of "high scores" that keep them so motivated and aligned with the company, they crack jokes about how they'd like to own it themselves some day.

In more conventional business settings, the only *immediate* feedback most workers receive is of the negative variety, calling their attention to mistakes or deficiencies. These employees often receive little or no positive feedback about their work whatsoever, at least not until the next quarter's results come out and show some improvement, or their regular performance appraisal meeting rolls around. By then it's old news—too little, too late—which keeps them so demotivated, they crack jokes about how they can't get away from the place fast enough at the end of each workday.

4. A High Level of Satisfaction As Scores Improve

"I win! Make mine two scoops of chocolate, please!"

Before any golf game begins, all the golfers involved know with complete certainty that they will not achieve a perfect score. But this knowledge does not weaken their determination to get as *close* to a perfect score as they possibly can. Serious golfers invest a small fortune in equipment and lessons and fees, along with untold hours of intense personal effort, all in order to become more skilled at sinking the little white balls into the little round holes in the ground. They consider the investment well worth it, because when their scores *do* improve, the feeling of accomplishment is *sooooo* intensely gratifying.

Serious bowlers, too, know beforehand that they won't succeed in knocking down every pin every time. But their efforts to do so remain undiminished. And any time they manage to get closer to the unattainable ideal, the air is full of shouts and cries and whoops and cheers. Just *watching* their exhilaration can be exhilarating.

The game at our donut store (and in other businesses with similarly strong internal alignment) is not to try and sink a hole-in-one every time, nor to knock down every pin every time. The game is to try and delight every customer every time. The players know beforehand that they won't achieve a perfect score—but this knowledge does nothing to deter them from trying. And their workplace has been set up to make the game enjoyable.

Bowling alleys and tennis courts are costly to build and maintain, golf courses even more so. These and many more such facilities can be found in almost every community, so that bored and frustrated workers (and other people too, of course) who hate their jobs have places to go to participate in satisfying activities.

At our Dunkin' Donuts store, the owners add extra staff to ensure that customers will be served quickly. This costs money. The equipment in the main store is duplicated in the drive-thru section, to make it easier for the workers to serve drive-thru customers well. And a second separate drive-thru lane is created, to further speed up the customer experience. This represents more costs. Bigger donut displays mean more fresh choices for customers, but also more throwaways at night. Another cost. In this business the game is customer delight, and the entire facility has been designed and set up for that purpose.

Bowlers and golfers must *pay* for the pleasure of playing their respective games in well-appointed facilities designed for that purpose. Employees at our store *get* paid to play their game in a well-appointed facility designed for that purpose.

Getting a high score in a game based on sinking white balls in holes or knocking white pins over can produce tremendous feelings of satisfaction. How much more deeply satisfying can it be to get a high score in a game based on brightening other people's lives, and making them happy? How much more satisfying can it be to recall that this is a game you get paid to play?

In every successful high-energy business I've visited over the past two decades, what I've observed without exception are owners and managers who *do in fact* pay their workers to have a good time—and understand that this is precisely why the job gets done, and gets done far better than in their competitors' less-motivated settings.

Making work feel more like play is one of the most powerful ways to turn up the motivational heat in any business setting. But there may be hidden demotivators built into your existing business culture that are even more powerful—cooling factors capable of neutralizing any heat being applied. Before there can be any lasting motivational benefit from turning work into an engaging play-like activity, the big employee demotivators must first be removed for good.

How to permanently eliminate the biggest employee demotivator of them all is the subject of the next chapter.

Notes

1. Lynne McLaughlin, co-owner, Dunkin' Donuts, interview with the author, July 24, 2006.
2. Sharon Holdcraft, co-owner, Dunkin' Donuts, interview with the author, July 24, 2006.
3. Lynne McLaughlin interview.
4. James B. Gallimore, interview with the author, July 24, 2006.
5. Lynne McLaughlin interview.
6. James B. Gallimore interview.
7. Dave Marden, interview with the author, July 24, 2006.
8. Ed MacEachern, interview with the author, July 24, 2006.
9. Dave Marden interview.
10. Ed MacEachern interview.
11. Dorothy Gallimore, interview with the author, July 24, 2006.
12. Lynne McLaughlin interview.
13. Dorothy Gallimore interview.
14. Sharon Holdcraft interview.
15. Lynne McLaughlin interview.
16. Sharon Holdcraft interview.
17. Tracy Brown, employee, Dunkin' Donuts, interview with the author, July 24, 2006.
18. Amy McCaul, employee, Dunkin' Donuts, interview with the author, July 24, 2006.

19. Joe Yousufi, interview with the author, from the video *Spectacular Service: A Question of Attitude*, International Tele-Film, 1995. Readers can view the entire interview at www.customerfocusbreakthroughs.com by clicking on Book Supplements/Video.

20. Mihaly Csikszentmihalyi, *Flow: The Psychology of Optimal Experience* (New York: Harper & Row, 1990).

21. Amy McCaul interview.

22. Tracy Brown interview.

23. Tracy Brown interview.

Chapter 2

The Biggest Demotivator

What the heck does "self-motivated" mean? The phrase appears in every second recruitment ad in every newspaper published in the past 50 years, so there are clearly an awful lot of people who believe they know exactly what it refers to—and who furthermore consider it *highly desirable*, whatever it means.

I must be some kind of blockhead. I know what "eager" means, for example, but if someone used the phrase "self-eager" I wouldn't really know what they were getting at. "Enthused," fine. But "self-enthused?" That I'd have trouble understanding. And I definitely know what "motivated" means. I've been observing highly motivated employees in action, and interviewing them in all kinds of business settings, and writing about them, for years.

But when I've asked these fired-up workers what it is that motivates them to work so hard, not one of them has ever said, "Oh, I motivate myself." To the contrary, without exception, they all attribute their on-the-job excitement and enthusiasm to something outside themselves, something in their workplace—or in the nature of the work itself—that somehow differentiates it from what most of their friends or family members do for a living.

Our object in this book is to get a handle on that particular motivational "something" that separates a small proportion of businesses from all the rest. We want to clarify what it is, where it comes from, how it can be created when it's absent, and how it can be sustained and intensified when it's present.

Now I will acknowledge, there are some especially resourceful and optimistic people who find motivation to give their best effort even in job situations everyone else finds intolerable. These, of course, are the kinds of people writers of recruitment ads are looking for. These are the ones everyone describes as "self-motivated." (Okay, so I knew what it meant all along. In fact, I even wrote an entire book on the subject of self-motivation in the pursuit of personal life goals.) The bad news for recruiters: not only will you have a hard time finding those exceedingly rare individuals who remain motivated even in dismal work settings, your emphasis on "self-motivation" may also be scaring a lot of good candidates away. It's like holding up a sign that says, "Around here we either consider employee motivation unimportant, or else we very simply have *no clue* about how to go about creating it for our workers. Either way, if you're applying for a job here you better be able to find some way to motivate yourself, because you'll certainly be getting no help from us in that regard."

By definition, motivated businesses are driven by a motive. But what *is* their motive? Is it the same basic motive in all high-energy businesses, regardless of industry, size, or location? If we can identify a single, powerful motive that all high-performance businesses have in common—and if we can furthermore confirm that this same motive is strikingly absent in virtually all low-energy demotivated businesses—then we may have found the fundamental source of employee motivation. Where would we begin our search for this fundamental source?

We could turn from the Jobs section of our newspaper to the front page.

Moved to Volunteer

Volunteer rates hit record numbers. This was the main headline on the front page of the July 7, 2006 edition of *USA Today*. The accompanying story described how people are applying to organizations like the Peace Corps and Volunteers in Service to America (VISTA) in greater numbers than ever before. The story quotes Joseph Almeida, a 23-year-old who at that time had just completed a year of volunteer service in New York City as a fifth-grade teacher in the Teach for America program. "We have a venue to make a difference," he says. "I know that we're collectively working to impact something."[1] Elizabeth Jones, 26, of Portland, Oregon, adds, "There's a lot of need in this world, and it wasn't doing anything in my heart to help make the rich people be richer."[2]

These remarks become quite illuminating when considered within the larger context of human motivation. Taken on its own, the whole phenomenon of volunteerism can seem puzzling—why would people volunteer to give of their time, talents, and energies in activities that can often be unpleasant or even dangerous? The sign in the photo is an actual recruitment notice for a volunteer fire department in Glocester, Rhode

Island. Why would *anyone* choose to sign up for something like this? It's not until we frame volunteerism within a larger understanding of motivation that it all begins to make sense—and sheds an important clue about the source of workplace motivation in particular.

One of the great pioneers in the study of human motivation was Abraham Maslow, famous for the "hierarchy of needs" model he first introduced in 1954. Maslow categorized all basic human needs as a five-tier progression, beginning with survival issues such as air, drink, food, sleep, etc., and proceeding through safety and security needs, social and "belongingness" needs (which includes belonging to a successful team or work group), the need for self-esteem and achievement, and finally the need for self-actualization and personal fulfillment.

Each tier in this model represents what humans of all ages and cultures need most urgently *once the needs in the previous tier have been met*. In other words, wherever an individual happens to fall in this progression at any point in his or her life, filling the next *unmet* need on the list will become a major preoccupation—which is to say, a major motive for that individual. This would of course also apply to entire groups of individuals. If we think of "the homeless" as a distinct group, for example, the daily actions of members of this group will be governed by certain unmet needs all individuals within the group have in common. These are basic needs this group does not, however, share with a different group called "the wealthy," who fall elsewhere on the progression and are thus motivated by a different set of needs from a different tier in the model.

Where do "employees" fit as a group in this model? Maslow places them in the "belongingness" tier, number three of five. It means once they feel part of a work group or team, the *next* unmet need on their list—that is, the one they will feel most motivated to meet—has to do with self-esteem and achievement. "Satisfaction of the self-esteem need," Maslow writes, "leads to feelings of self-confidence, worth, strength, capability, and adequacy, of being useful and necessary in the world."[3]

Virtually all employees, as a distinct group, will find themselves preoccupied by the same "next unmet need": the need for a sense of "worth," the need to feel "useful and necessary in the world." When this basic need goes unmet in the workplace, workers often go searching for opportunities to fill it elsewhere. Thus we have well-paid lawyers who donate some of their time and expertise to members of the community unable to pay legal fees, and medical professionals who make themselves available to the needy at no charge. And we have workers from every kind of organization who derive no real sense of accomplishment and satisfaction from their regular jobs, and so volunteer to man crisis phone lines, or raise funds for this or that civic initiative, or otherwise help other people in some way outside of the workplace.

People volunteer to do all kinds of unpleasant and even dangerous things for no pay, precisely because these represent ways of helping others—and thus of meeting their own basic human need to feel useful and necessary in the world. As in the *USA Today* story, volunteers seek to "make a difference," to "impact something." "There's a lot of need in this world," as one volunteer put it, and "it wasn't doing anything in [her] heart to help make the rich people be richer."

Filling a need in the world vs. making the rich richer. There's the whole crux of the matter spelled out right there.

We're Working to Help Who, Again?

It may seem so basic a question it barely deserves a moment's thought—but in reality it may qualify as one of the ultimate make-it-or-break-it questions when it comes to employee motivation. It has to do with *purpose* at its most fundamental level. Tick off the box that best describes the current situation in your organization:

❑ My employees believe this business exists primarily to make piles of money. They believe management's view is that if we're also filling some human need out there, all the better.

❑ My employees believe this business exists primarily to fill some human need out there. They believe management's view is that if we're also making piles of money, all the better.

This simple either/or proposition gets to the very heart of the whole motivation issue. The notion that some businesses might consider profit as no more than a secondary benefit of their operation will naturally strike some owners and managers as preposterous. This will be especially true for those in business settings where employee cynicism and demotivation are rampant, and where (as a consequence) the drive for profitability is an all-consuming round-the-clock struggle for survival. (It's one of the greatest ironies in business—the handful of organizations that *don't* make profit their primary focus are very often the ones with the highest levels of employee motivation, and thus the highest profits as a direct result!)[4]

In the vast majority of business settings, what employees see every day is management's obsessive preoccupation with earnings, and with the general welfare of management itself. Processes, procedures, and policies are put in place for the convenience and benefit of the leadership team. The way it looks to workers, everything everyone does on the job every day is predicated on improving the bottom line, and thereby helping the highest-paid individuals at the top of the organizational chart secure whatever hefty bonuses and promotions they happen to be aiming for. This is an entire organizational culture devoted to helping "make the rich people be richer," an endeavor that never resonates very deeply in the hearts of most employees.

It's important to appreciate the *full extent* of the damage this kind of internal focus on self-interest does to employee motivation. Many business-people use a single word to describe the combined symptoms of demotivation, apathy, resistance to change, resentment, and mistrust on the part of their workers: they use the word *cynicism*. Good word, it says it all. In functional terms, employee cynicism is about as far away from employee motivation as you can get—the two are at opposite ends of the spectrum, poles apart. And where does employee cynicism come from? As the dictionary reminds us, the word refers to the belief that "human conduct [in this case, management conduct] is motivated wholly by self-interest." Ooops—there's that "self-interest" thing again. In any workplace, employee cynicism is *by definition* the shared belief that the organization is driven primarily by self-interest. It's pretty easy for workers to cultivate such a belief when all around them day after day they see and hear indisputable evidence that it's true.

Just how severe is the cynicism problem in our organizations? Severe enough, in the opinion of retail consultant Cheryl Beall*, that even throwing money at employees doesn't help. "I've been involved in a lot of organizations that are changing compensation structures," she explains, "and the company will come out and tell [their employees], very clearly, that, 'Oh, we're gonna give you this new comp structure, this is going to be great, these are all the reasons why it's going to help you.' But I believe that there's such a level of employee cynicism, as soon as they hear [their company is] changing the comp structure, they immediately decide, 'Well this can't possibly have a ben-efit for me. The only reason the company would be changing this is because, you know, it's going to save them money, and they're going to be stealing something from me.'" This is cynicism of a high order, all right—but is it real-ly commonplace? "I've helped several clients do a complete comp change," Cheryl says, "and that always comes out."[5]

As soon as managers begin to notice cynicism going up—and therefore motivation going down—they typically set about trying to correct the problem. In most cases they do so by prescribing what is altogether the wrong medicine. Operating on the assumption that employees are forever looking for an answer to *What's In It For Me?*, they decide it's going to be necessary to cut their workers a bigger slice of the action. Thus begins the endless cycle of pay raises and employee incentives and cash prizes and bonuses, all intended to transform cynicism back into motivation.

Not only are such measures ineffective cynicism-reducers, over the longer term they can actually become cynicism-*intensifiers*. As employees resign themselves to the fact that their work is never going to become a source of personal fulfillment—is never going to give them a reason to feel "useful and necessary in the world"—they often adopt a "might as well at least get all I can out of this place while I'm stuck here anyway" attitude.

Their new motive becomes to wheedle as many cash prizes and incen-tives for themselves as possible, usually while doing as little as possible to

---

* During her 18 years in luxury retail, Cheryl Beall held positions such as store manager, VP of retail, and director of stores in such organizations as Bergdorf Goodman, Loro Piana, Hermes, and Mont Blanc. She became "store doctor" for Luca Luca in Las Vegas, helping them put together their marketing strategies, and two years ago established Retail 101, her own New-York based consulting firm. She's the author of *Taking The 'I' Out of Clientele: A Retailer's Guide To Selling Better Than You Can Sell*.

earn them. By that point they *are* looking for what's-in-it-for-them, just as their managers had originally assumed. By then the culture of self-interest has trickled down from the top of the organization to every level of the operation. And of course by then the concerns of external parties (such as customers) have become an entirely secondary consideration.

The single biggest employee demotivator of them all is a predominant organizational focus on self-interest. This is the very wellspring of employee cynicism. And cynicism is the antithesis of motivation. A predominant focus on self-interest is the supreme cultural cooling factor that quickly overwhelms and cancels out any and all subsequent motivational heating factors that may be brought into play.

This would seem to create quite a dilemma. Obviously, no business can afford to think of profit and growth as anything less than *absolutely essential* for its survival. Survival is self-interest in its most basic form; encouraging everyone to begin treating it as unimportant would be tantamount to committing organizational suicide. Yet at the same time, profit and growth in business are virtually unachievable without a motivated workforce—and a preoccupation with this kind of self-interest tends to reduce (and can even completely destroy) employee motivation.

Is there any way out of this dilemma?

There is. As suggested above, the organization must replace the pursuit of profit with the pursuit of something else—but something that *as an inevitable result* will also increase profits even more dramatically. The entire organization must shift its focus from inward to outward. It must become more preoccupied with helping others than with helping itself. It must give employees, as a routine part of their jobs, frequent opportunities to feel they're doing something meaningful and worthwhile for others outside the organization. It must stop looking for answers to what's-in-it-for-me, and instead begin delivering answers to why-should-I-care. To boil all of this down to its simplest terms, the organization must begin giving its workers a *reason to care* about what the business stands for, and what it's striving to accomplish.

But is there a reasonably quick and easy way to engineer so profound a shift of cultural focus?

There is. And, perhaps surprisingly, it does *not* involve customer service.

The Wrong-Way Door to Enlightenment

I was once sitting in the lobby of a small hotel, awaiting the arrival of a colleague. I had some reading material but found it hard to concentrate—there was a sudden clattering noise that filled the lobby at irregular intervals. I looked around to find the source of this irritating racket, but all would fall silent whenever I searched for it, and then of course the noise would occur again the moment I'd resumed my reading. Eventually, in exasperation, I took a longer break from reading and began scanning all corners of the lobby for the cause of this increasingly annoying sound. And finally I found it.

The glass-and-metal front door was the culprit. The door was slightly higher than street level, which meant people entering the hotel had to climb two small concrete steps, and without exception they then assumed the door was designed to be *pushed* open. Not so. The annoying noise was the rattle of the metallic door clanging against its metallic frame. I suddenly remembered my own experience the day before—I too had first tried to push the hotel door open (and had no doubt distracted anyone in the lobby trying to read), and then realized I had to actually move backwards and *step back down* one of the two steps in order to create enough room to *pull* the door open wide enough to enter. Particularly inconvenient for people with baggage or parcels.

As I was reviewing this in my mind, the door made a particularly loud and jarring rattle as someone tried to push it open—so much so that even the gentleman behind the front counter raised his eyes. He saw I was looking his way. "They all do that," he said, smiling and shaking his head. "Nobody reads signs any more." And with that he resumed his work at the counter.

Signs? What was he referring to? I could see no sign on the door when the arriving visitor pulled it open to enter.

That evening, rushing back into the hotel to get out of the cold, I once again pushed the door without thinking, and created a loud clatter against the frame. I remembered to pull the handle instead, and this time noticed the word PULL painted on it. This must have been the sign the attendant had referred to earlier, the sign nobody reads.

This incident took place early in my career, but (as you can see) it made a lasting impression. It stayed with me because it was an intriguing example of something I at first had some trouble getting my head around—a clear-cut failure to meet customer expectations, yet one that could not in any way be described as "poor customer service." If anything, the staff at this hotel actually delivered very *good* customer service. But that annoying door ...

Here's another case to consider, also (purely by coincidence) hotel-related. When I'm speaking to larger groups of business people who do a fair amount of traveling, I sometimes ask this question: show of hands—how many of you have ever been awakened by a hotel wake-up call that *you did not request*? Typically a lot of hands go up. Part two of the question: when this *doesn't* happen—when your sleep is *not* interrupted needlessly—do you later think of this as an example of "good customer service?" Along similar lines, would it ever occur to you to compliment a hotel on its "good customer service" because the batteries in the TV remote control were not dead, or the bulbs in the bedside lamps were not burned out?

All of these represent examples of customer expectations being met, yet none of them have anything to do with what most people think of as customer service. This is what the wrong-way door helped me understand many years ago. Customer service is only the tip of a huge iceberg—the smaller, more visible part of the equation that customers see in their direct encounters with frontline workers. Lurking below the surface is the much larger issue of *customer focus*. This is the less visible behind-the-scenes part, the part that *managers* are responsible for. If batteries and light bulbs are routinely checked and replaced, it's because a *process* has been put in place by management to ensure this consistently gets done. If guests are awakened by wake-up calls they did not request, it means management at that hotel has failed to put a *process* in place to ensure that such requests are canceled when guests check out. An awkward door that makes an annoying noise will continue to do so until some customer-focused manager decides correcting the situation will be a good investment in improving the customer experience.

There was nothing wrong with the level of service at the hotel with the wrong-way door, yet as a customer I still came away with no urge ever to return. Back then my understanding of the relationship between customer service and customer focus was not yet fully developed—all I knew was a nearby competitor delivered a similar level of customer service and did *not* have an annoying wrong-way door, and that alone was reason enough for me to take my business elsewhere.

The lesson of the wrong-way door: when it comes to gaining competitive advantage through delivery of a superior customer experience, improving customer service is actually the smaller part of the challenge. "Service" is the part that lies within the realm and control of frontline workers. The far bigger part involves improving customer focus—that is, creating a culture across the whole organization where *everyone at all levels* becomes equally preoccupied with finding ways to improve every aspect of the customer experience. Focus is the part that falls within the realm and control of managers. Many businesses make a heavy investment in costly training programs designed to improve the smaller employee-based service element; few invest anything at all in formal efforts to improve the far larger management-based focus element.

The question that began this account of the wrong-way door was whether there existed a reasonably quick and easy way to profoundly shift an organization's cultural focus. Specifically, because employee cynicism is the inevitable result of an organization's internal focus on self-interest, what we're looking for is a cultural shift *outward*, one that will appeal to workers' deep-seated need to feel they're making a positive difference for somebody out there in the world. Our interest is in a quick and easy cultural shift that will replace cynicism with motivation, apathy with enthusiasm—and will also directly improve profitability by generating a powerful competitive advantage. A tall order.

There is only one kind of culture change that can meet every one of these criteria at the same time. It is a shift to a customer-focused culture, yes—but not to just any kind of customer-focused culture. This is one of a specific kind, one with an important difference.

The Flashpoint Culture

It may seem a bit peculiar, discussing customer focus in a book about employee motivation. But it wouldn't seem peculiar at all to people who work in one particular kind of business operation.

Almost every community has at least one "famous" local business—famous for how busy it always is, how friendly its staff is, how superior its service is. Imagine if we could somehow magically transplant the best of these from all over the continent into a single community. We'd pick the one most energized, most popular business from a list of categories (bakery, car dealership, supermarket, taxi company, insurance provider, department store, real estate office, etc.) and then set them all up next door to each other along a cluster of streets, and create a commercial district like no other on the planet. Managers would be able to visit this remarkable place and go from door to door to observe and ask questions and learn. They'd want to discover those elements that all such businesses have in common, and try to figure out how to import some of these elements into their own business operations back home.

Common elements—that's what I've wanted to discover over the years as well. But because no such grouping of super-businesses of this type exists in any one location, I've had to do it the hard way. Fortunately my work with business clients all over the map has given me ample opportunity to travel, and whenever possible I've made a point of finding out where the "star performers" were in various localities. I've been allowed to observe and ask questions and learn. (Examples of some of the answers to my questions appear in these pages.) And I've been able to isolate the common elements that all such businesses share, regardless of their size and industry and location.

Foremost among the elements most such businesses share is one especially striking cultural characteristic that almost never applies in mainstream business organizations: *"employee motivation" and "customer satisfaction" are treated as a single issue.* That is, these businesses continually find new ways to delight customers precisely because they know this is also the best way to keep their employees energized.

So intense is their collective determination to consistently deliver a superior customer experience, these organizations often adopt what could look to mainstream managers like an almost not-for-profit approach to business. One "wow factor" extra is piled onto another, one more value-add is thrown in here, one more freebie or discount is added there, until anyone keeping track with a calculator might begin to worry for their fiscal health. And yet—that old paradox again—these businesses are almost invariably the biggest moneymakers in their respective markets. How this is possible only becomes clear when we dig a little deeper and begin to observe the many ways such an approach dramatically lowers almost all the basic costs of running a business. In particular, marketing costs (associated with attracting new customers to replace defectors who don't return) and turnover costs (associated with attracting and training new employees to replace defectors who don't return) are often all but absent in such operations.

This almost-philanthropic approach to customer satisfaction has an extremely powerful effect on workers in such organizations. The employees find it deeply satisfying to know they are part of a group effort to delight customers, to help customers, to make customers' lives brighter or simpler or happier in some way. It's to accomplish precisely such things that people choose to become volunteers—but these kinds of businesses *pay* workers to accomplish them as part of their regular workday. And as we'll see later, this motivational effect is even further amplified when it's the workers' own ideas or initiatives that are responsible for the high levels of customer satisfaction.

If an internal focus on organizational self-interest is the primary cultural "cooling factor" that destroys motivation in most other business settings, here it is conversely the external focus on the interests of customers that drive motivational temperatures skyward. The cultural dynamics are not complicated, but they are unique to businesses of this kind.

Track with me—here's the simplest way to sum up the cultural forces involved. In the first place, customers always prefer dealing with enthusiastic, fired-up employees; the high level of worker motivation becomes a source of customer satisfaction in and of itself. But beyond this, as the customer experience unfolds, the various additional elements of delight will typically inspire these customers to express their appreciation in one way or another. And this kind of spontaneous positive feedback from people outside the organization tends to have a profoundly motivational effect on the workers.

There's a kind of chain reaction that kicks in: employee motivation drives up customer satisfaction, and appreciation from satisfied customers in turn drives up employee motivation. The two elements eventually begin to fuel each other to the point where they become fused. The organization experiences a flashpoint of contagious energy and enthusiasm.

This flashpoint effect therefore represents both employee motivation and customer satisfaction at their highest possible level. But what may be less immediately obvious is that the two are co-dependent: *neither can reach so high a level without the other doing the same in tandem.*

None of this is a particularly complicated idea—and yet only a very small minority of businesses understand it, and even fewer ever succeed in applying it. Most mainstream businesses continue to attack problems related to employee motivation and customer satisfaction as two separate issues, each with their own expensive (and ineffective) remedies.

The traditional remedy for low employee motivation, as we've seen, involves so-called incentive programs in one form or another. These seldom produce real and lasting benefits and can often end up worsening the problem.

The traditional remedy for low customer satisfaction is customer service training in one form or another. The object of most such training is to present workers with a list of "desired behaviors" and then attempt to somehow coax or cajole or bully participants into adopting these behaviors in the workplace. Here too, the overall success rate has been dismal. Employees sarcastically refer to such programs as "smile training" and tend to resent the implication that it is they who are mainly responsible for customer dissatisfaction, and it is therefore they who need to be "fixed" through such training. It's as true in our homes and schools as it is in our workplaces—showing people how we want them to behave, without creating within them any actual desire (that is, motive) to do so, will almost invariably lead to stiff resistance and will almost invariably produce disappointing results over the long term.

To recap key points covered thus far—two cultural characteristics most highly-motivated businesses have in common:

1. As described in Chapter One, **they make work feel more like play.** (We'll be looking at the best way to accomplish this shortly.)
2. As outlined in this chapter, **they exhibit a predominantly outward focus on the interests and welfare of customers.** (This is their antidote to employee cynicism. It's the one primary "motive" that drives everything they do, the fundamental source of their motivation. There'll be more on creating this kind of shared focus in subsequent chapters.)

Bringing energy into focus creates an extremely powerful force for change. In a meadow, on a pleasant summer day, the sun spreads just enough warmth and light to create a comfortable environment in which plants and animals can thrive. But if a child uses a simple magnifying lens to *focus* some of the sun's rays down to a single small spot, in a matter of seconds a wisp of smoke appears, and soon a lick of flame, and then a small fire that can quickly become a major blaze. All living things in the meadow must flee or perish. The entire environment is transformed from comfortable to deadly in a matter of moments.

So, in business settings, is focusing primarily on customers—while also making work feel more life play—a combination powerful enough to ignite a flashpoint chain reaction?

Almost, but not quite. The two in combination are enough to replace employee cynicism with enthusiasm, which for many struggling businesses may already seem a dream come true. But the flashpoint effect requires motivation at the highest possible level. It's a little like a three-legged stool, and so far we've only dealt with two legs.

In the third chapter we discuss the third—and perhaps most powerful—way to inject a compelling personal "motive" into employee motivation.

Notes

1. "Volunteer rates hit record numbers," *USA Today*, July 7, 2006.
2. Ibid.
3. Abraham H. Maslow, *Motivation and Personality*, 2nd. ed. (New York, Harper & Row, 1970).
4. There's more about this "Profit Paradox" in Paul Levesque, *Customer Service Made Easy* (Entrepreneur Press, 2006), including the following references:

   "Contrary to business school doctrine ... 'profit maximization' has not been the dominant driving force or primary objective through the history of the visionary companies.... Yes, they seek profits, but they're equally guided by a core ideology—core values and sense of purpose beyond just making money. Yet, paradoxically, the visionary companies make more money than the more purely profit-driven comparison companies."

> —James C. Collins and Jerry I. Porras
> *Built To Last: Successful Habits of Visionary Companies* (New York: HarperBusiness, 1994).

"Companies that do make a lot of money almost never have as their goal 'making a lot of money.'"

> —From the chapter "The Primary Purpose of Business is Not To Make Money" in Robert A. Lutz [chairman of General Motors North America], *Guts: 8 Laws of Business from One of the Most Innovative Business Leaders of Our Time* (Hoboken, NJ: John Wiley & Sons Inc., 1998).

5. Cheryl Beall, Retail 101, interview with the author, October 20, 2006.

Chapter 3

Getting the Culture Shift Started

"I believe that people want a leader," says retail consultant Cheryl Beall. "Even if they're leaders themselves. They want to believe that there's a place to go, that there's a purpose, that somebody has an objective. People love to buy into that."

Cheryl illustrates her point with a story from her days as a store manager at Bergdorf Goodman. "My favorite thing was always the cashmere sale, right before Thanksgiving. When [business] was slow I would always go to the third floor and get a stack of cashmere sweaters, and I would go march around the whole store. We had seven floors. So I'm walking around with this huge stack of cashmere sweaters—as though I'm on my way someplace—and I had more people come and say to me, 'Oh my gosh, what's going on, where are those?'" Cheryl reenacts the way she would pause in her purposeful march to turn to the customer, as if caught slightly off-guard by the question. "'Oh—yeah, they're on the third floor, we're having this great sale.'"[1]

We've all experienced something like this. We've seen how anyone moving with determination and purpose attracts attention—whether in a particular place on a particular occasion, or in life generally. We've seen how a crowd tends to draw a crowd, even to the point where individuals can sometimes become swept up in a mob and behave in ways that would otherwise be utterly alien to them. We've been at busy theme parks or checkout counters and seen people take their place in line without thinking, even when an adjoining point of entry or exit clearly has no line at all. We all know of "trendy" restaurants or clubs that seem to be popular precisely because they're known for being popular. (As Yogi Berra famously said of one such place, "Nobody goes there anymore; it's too crowded.")

What is this mysterious force that attracts people, that motivates them to move in the same direction that others are moving? What's creating the pull?

Pulling Together

Young science students learn about the pull of a magnetic field by sprinkling iron filings at random, like pepper, on a white sheet of paper. When a magnet is positioned under the paper, many of the individual specks of iron shift slightly along the axis of the magnetic field. Though the motion of each individual particle is slight, the overall pattern they create on the paper becomes strikingly different. Instead of a random distribution of little black specks, the students see a clear series of lines that extend from one of the magnet's poles to the other, with greater concentrations of filings where the magnetic pull is strongest. A "map" of the entire magnetic field becomes clearly visible.

Anyone who enjoys reading biographies will be well acquainted with the way individuals driven by a powerful sense of purpose exert a similar kind of pull on others around them. The best-known examples are the great leaders, who have always had an almost magical ability to attract supporters, and even to turn critics into collaborators. Though smaller-scale examples of the same principle may not be as widely-known, they are nevertheless all around us.

The moment we learn that someone is "on a mission," or is aspiring to accomplish something difficult, our interest is captured. At first, we're simply curious: will they succeed? But if they don't let setbacks discourage them, if they don't give up, if they manage to continue moving closer and closer to their goal, our curiosity turns into outright *support*. The closer they get to success, the more we want to *see* them succeed. We find cheering their progress exhilarating. And we find their ultimate triumph inspiring.

People who aspire to do the difficult—people driven by a purpose—create what we can think of as an "aspirational field" around themselves. On a day-by-day basis they, like everybody else, find themselves having to deal with a seemingly endless list of random and unrelated details. But gradually they begin to see a pattern where none was visible before. They begin to see with increasing clarity how all of these random elements relate either directly or indirectly to their greater purpose. All of the random elements of their lives seem to shift ever so slightly, like iron filings, until they all seem pointed in a single direction, along the axis of their aspiration.

When we take a careful look at the lives of people on a mission, we see this alignment effect over and over again. The individual aspiring to become a published novelist always considered mowing the lawn or doing the laundry a huge distraction, until he or she discovered that this activity afforded a perfect opportunity to clear the mind and work out complicated plot points. The commuter determined to learn a second language uses a recorded program that turns the formerly despised commuting time into a productive and satisfying part of the day. In example after example, the energy of the aspiration pulls random elements of life into alignment.[2]

The alignment effect of the aspirational field is even more strikingly apparent in *collective* human endeavors, such as in military teams, or sports teams, or business teams. A shared aspiration is one of the great motivators, powerful enough to move individuals to heights of achievement that often far surpass what they themselves considered the limits of their ability. Speak to anyone who at any point in their lives was part of a group effort to achieve something difficult, something they believed in, and almost certainly the word "inspirational" will come up. The leader was inspirational, or the cause itself was inspirational, or the shared triumph of success was inspirational. These are the episodes in people's lives that make them misty-eyed in the recounting. These are the moments many look back on as the high-water mark in their whole life experience, moments they find themselves reliving in cherished memory for the rest of their days.

We find a great many examples of this kind of deep feeling in the history of business, especially within organizations under the leadership of "pioneers." These visionary leaders were determined to create a new kind of industry, a new technology, a new and better way of doing things. Their passion was contagious—or, to put it another way, they created a powerful aspirational field around themselves that drew others into alignment with their objective. The organizations created by such leaders typically later turn their founders into figures of folklore with almost superhuman characteristics. These are organizations that worry they cannot possibly survive after their leader—the source of all their inspiration—dies or retires (even though their aspirational field usually proves strong enough to withstand even this). It's from organizations of this kind that former employees cannot share stories of "the early days" without developing a faraway look in their eyes and a lump in their throats. There are just simply not many things in this life quite so moving—in every sense of the word—as being part of a shared objective that everyone involved is determined to see realized.

A Culture In Alignment

ASPIRE TO INSPIRE BEFORE YOU EXPIRE, as the saying goes. Not, apparently, a piece of advice most business managers have taken to heart. Few workplaces can boast of employees who consistently report feeling "inspired" by the work they do, or by the bosses under whose thumbs they find themselves doing it.

In cultural terms, where the governing principle in a business setting is profit and self-interest, the organization as a whole will almost inevitably find itself being pulled in a multitude of directions at once, in pursuit of different—and frequently conflicting—priorities. This is because even when everyone at the top believes they're all striving for the same improvement in the profit picture, as individuals driven by self-interest they'll each have a way of getting there that works better for *them*. The head of marketing, for example, may be pressing to improve profits by investing more in promotion and advertising, while at the same time the head of finance is striving to improve profits by doing the exact opposite, cutting all unnecessary spending to the bone. (Discussions between these two may generate a few sparks.)

The "pulled in all directions" problem doesn't stop at the top. When you zoom in for a closer look at the next level down, you'll typically find individual managers similarly working against each other to "outshine" their peers. Each hopes to be perceived as head of the department or team doing most to improve profits, and thus the one most eligible for juicy bonuses and promotions. If one department's pursuit of glory causes the accomplishments of another to be reduced or even negated, well, this is an unfortunate but necessary evil in a culture dominated by self-interest.

Continue to zoom in for closer views, and it's the same story right down to the level of individual workers. Everybody's got his or her own personal every-man-for-himself, cover-your-rear-end set of priorities. Cultures of self-interest are characterized not only by cynicism on the rise, but also by alignment on the decline.

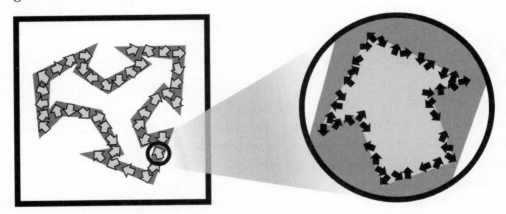

"Without alignment you've got so much segregation that you just don't get good work accomplished," says Brian Gallagher*, Director of Store Operations and Administration for the hundred-plus U.S.-based stores of Swiss chocolatier Lindt & Sprüngli. "You're doing work two or three times, and getting different answers, because you're wanting to look at it for *your* reason, and somebody else wants to look at it for *their* reason.

Getting common answers is hard enough, let alone then coming up with solutions to those questions."[3]

Organizations with cultural alignment present a strikingly different picture. No matter how far down you zoom in, everyone and everything is still pointing in the same single direction. There's an old story (perhaps apocryphal) that shortly after articulating his vision of "landing a man on the moon and returning him safely to the Earth," President Kennedy was visiting the newly-constructed facilities of the space agency, where he encountered a janitor sweeping the floor. "And what do you do here?" the president asked. "I'm helping put a man on the moon, sir," the janitor replied. Now that's the kind of top-to-bottom alignment that gets difficult missions accomplished.

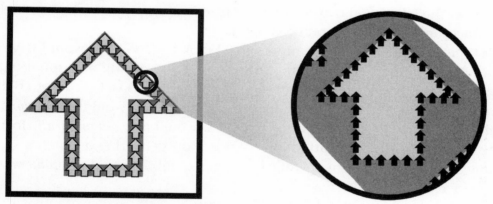

As Brian Gallagher puts it, "When there's a common understanding of what the ultimate goal is, there's nobody in any group of people who has to question what it is you're trying to accomplish. Any time you have to talk about what it is you're trying to accomplish in a business setting, that's a *complicated discussion*. But once that is ironed out and understood, and

* Before joining Lindt & Sprüngli at their Stratham, New Hampshire home office, Brian Gallagher spent five years at Crabtree & Evelyn, first as Director of Store Operations, then as Director of Sales. Depending on the time of year, the U.S. subsidiary of Lindt & Sprüngli Switzerland ("Master chocolatier since 1845") employs between 750 and 1,000 employees in its retail stores, with an additional 250 to 500 at the home office, which also has a manufacturing operation.

everyone's in alignment, the support levels are higher.... And when you do have failures, it's not a *person's* failure. The company tried to do something for the right reason, and you live and you learn, and you do it better the next time."[4]

So doesn't the quest for higher profits qualify as the kind of worthy "ultimate goal" Brian refers to, the kind that can create organization-wide alignment? It doesn't, because it's something that only really matters to a small part of the employee population (upper management). Similarly, although both *making work feel more like play* (Chapter One) and *focusing more on customer needs* (Chapter Two) represent solid motivational strategies, neither strategy will involve everyone at every level of the organization. The former would qualify more as a management-level initiative, whereas the latter would apply more to frontline employees who routinely interact directly with external customers.

What would an ideal "common goal" look like? Well, it would have a strong aspirational component, strong enough to create an aspirational field with the power to shift alignment from the executive boardroom right down to the level of every individual employee. Plus, it would also *automatically* make work feel more like play. Plus, it would also *automatically* focus the entire organization's attention outward, on delivering a superior customer experience. And as the biggest bonus of all, it would also *automatically* increase profits.

Where would you find a "single common goal" that can achieve all that? Well, if your organization happens to have a boardroom, and if in that room there happens to be a framed mission statement hanging on the wall—well, that's one place you almost certainly *won't* find it.

The Shocking Truth About Your Mission Statement

Does your business already have a formal mission statement? If so, take this simple ten-second test to determine whether it's serving any useful purpose whatsoever.

Question 1: When you think about your business, what's the number-one problem or objective that currently keeps you awake at night?

Question 2: Is solving that particular problem or achieving that particular objective the central element of your current mission statement?

If not, that thing you *call* a mission statement is in all probability something else altogether. In my two decades-plus of working with businesses of all sizes and types all over the world, I've had occasion to see quite a few attractively framed so-called mission statements. So far, I've encountered only a very small handful that describe any kind of actual mission. Almost without exception, these framed statements are declarations of what line of work the business is in, along with a sprinkling of generalities about how the business prefers to do business. If there's any aspirational element to the statement at all—many have none—it usually revolves around becoming the best in the field some day, becoming the "premiere supplier" or the "preferred employer," or the "customers' first choice." Nothing wrong with dreaming about becoming leader of the pack some day, of course; but if nothing concrete is being done to make that specific dream a reality, the chances of it happening are not encouraging. These are not missions— they're descriptions of what things would be like *after the fact*, if an aspirational mission of some kind were actually achieved.

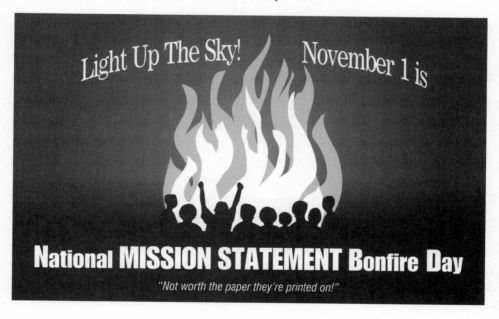

The huge disadvantage of typical mission statements is that they can mislead the entire management team into believing their business is on a mission of at least *some* kind, where in fact no real mission exists. When management observes widespread apathy for the so-called mission, they'll often be inclined to conclude it can only mean all employees are by nature a cynical, demotivated, lethargic bunch to begin with. Not convinced there's apathy around your current mission statement? It's easy to find out: invite any 10 randomly chosen workers to rattle it off from memory, and multiply the score by 10 to convert it into a percentage. A final score in the zero-percent range would suggest the possible presence of apathy.

Here's the clincher: in virtually every high-energy flashpoint business I know of, there's *no formal mission statement whatsoever*. These businesses don't need a mission statement to clarify what they're striving to accomplish. This is what cultural alignment actually means—everyone is crystal-clear about what objective they're aligned to. Asking 10 randomly chosen workers to summarize their common goal in this kind of business setting will virtually always yield a score in the hundred-percent range.

So the kind of goal that fosters organization-wide alignment typically has little in common with the sorts of points that appear under the heading "Mission Statement." What else can we discover about such goals?

Everybody Sing: E-I-E-I-O

"The way you get around cynicism," says Cheryl Beall, "is to involve the employees in developing their own solutions."[5]

Brian Gallagher of Lindt & Sprüngli concurs: "It probably causes you to spend two to three times more energy getting something done when you don't involve the field and the home office from the get-go."[6]

Beth Guastella,* senior vice president of retail in the Kate Spade chain of

---

* Beth Guastella's entire 21-year career has been in the "luxury goods business." She was with Hermes for eight years and with Mont Blanc for five prior to joining Kate Spade. At the time of our interview there were 19 full-price Kate Spade stores across the U.S., along with four outlet stores and one Jack Spade store. We spoke on what happened to be the final day of Beth's nearly four years with Kate Spade; she has since assumed the position of President of Retail at New York's Stuart Weitzman.

luxury stores, cites employees "feeling challenged and stimulated in their work world" as a basic source of motivation. "In kind of mapping out the year, we do this exercise [that we call] roadmap," she explains. "It's very participatory.... I take a conference room, I put the flip chart papers around, and there's one chart for every month, and we use colored post-it notes.... in order to kind of map out our year, physically map it out, of what all is going to have to happen. They all do it. I participate in it, but they all do it. And then I have them each get up there and talk about what is going to happen.... Basically it becomes the roadmap, but it's something that I didn't create, *they* created it. And with that I certainly get much bigger buy-in."

But what if the group fails to identify a particular item Beth wants to see accomplished? "As they're working through this," she says, "if I see that they're missing something ... that could be rather important to our business, then I would ... prompt them a little bit.... Even with prompting, if I'm able to have them come to the conclusion of what it is we want to achieve, then there's greater ownership, there's buy-in to that particular concept. So then because it's *their* concept, not my concept, then they will certainly carry that through."[7]

"I think it's very powerful that our service standards were organically grown," says Stewart Collins,* Director of Standards and Quality Assurance in the Parks & Resorts division of Delaware North Companies (DNC), one of the largest privately owned companies in the U.S. "And I use the word 'organic' very deliberately," he adds, emphasizing that he prefers it to the more common term "home-grown," which, he says, "gives at least to me the connotations of that mom-and-pop country-bumpkin kind of thing."

Stewart is referring to the service standards associated with DNC's *GuestPath* program—which, as we'll see in more detail later, is a superb example of a multifaceted culture-shaping initiative that creates powerful alignment across his entire company. "*GuestPath* is an organically grown

---

* Stewart Collins was in his seventh year with Delaware North Companies (DNC) at the time of our interview. The company has been in existence for over 90 years. It owns a number of resorts, operates a number more on a management contract basis, and is also a concessionaire in a number of properties. The company's revenues are approaching $2 billion annually. It has 40,000 associates serving half a billion customers in the U.S., Canada, the U.K., Australia, and New Zealand.

program," he repeats, "and I can't overemphasize the importance of that for us. That organic process of going through the pain of figuring out what those ten 'universal standards' were going to be was so powerful—even though the standards themselves are so simple."8

It's the same pattern in every turbo-charged flashpoint business you care to visit—management gets employees directly involved in planning and implementing their own ideas to improve the operation or the customer experience. Their *own* ideas, "own" as in "ownership." Employee involvement and ownership. EIO. It's the magic bullet, the missing piece, the third leg of our motivation strategy, the final aspect that binds all the other aspects together. It provides employees at all levels with the best possible answer to the question *Why Should I Care?* I care because it happens to be *my idea*, and I want to see my idea succeed. It's a reflection of what I believe in and who I am.

To put it all into context, the three differentiating characteristics of all highly motivated (and therefore culturally aligned) businesses are:

1. **To the employees who work there, work feels more like play.**
   - There's a challenging goal or objective.
   - Players understand the rules and how the game is to be played.
   - There's a scoring mechanism that provides immediate feedback.
   - There's celebration and recognition for every win.

2. **The organization is customer-focused, rather than profit-focused.**
   - An outward focus on filling customers' needs reduces cynicism, the inevitable by-product of an inward focus on self-interest.
   - Delivering a delightful experience to customers gives workers an opportunity to feel "useful and necessary in the world," feelings that make work satisfying and fulfilling.
   - Positive feedback from happy customers is profoundly motivational to workers.

3. **Employees are allowed to experience high levels of involvement and ownership.**
   - Workers don't feel pressured to pursue a goal they think of as belonging to management; the goal is very much their own.
   - A single shared goal creates organization-wide alignment.

When we bring the complete big picture together, we're at last in a position to define the ideal goal—the kind of goal that can generate an aspirational field powerful enough to bring the culture of any organization into total alignment.

Remember, we're looking for a goal that will be equally meaningful to everyone across the entire organization, and will also at the same time make work feel more like play for employees, and will also focus the organization's attention on delivering a superior customer experience, and will also improve bottom-line results. It may seem inconceivable that a single goal could accomplish all this—but there is one goal that can.

One way to phrase such a goal might be *employees devise and implement their own strategies for gaining competitive advantage through delivery of a superior customer experience.* Too big a mouthful? How's this: *employees come up with ideas to delight customers and steal business from the competition.* Still too wordy? Okay, how about, *employees figure out ways to win customers from competitors.*

Fact is, the actual wording is not particularly important. What's important is for the goal to incorporate three elements. First, as in play activities, there should be rivals for us to outplay, rivals *outside* the organization, like our competitors—a "common enemy" to unite us in a challenge we all share and believe in. Second, as in volunteer work, there should be a strong sense that others outside the organization (especially our customers) are genuinely benefiting in some meaningful way from our efforts. And third, as in any truly collaborative undertaking, we should all be involved to at least some extent in the planning and execution of the shared objective, and in the triumph whenever we succeed.

The wording of the goal is secondary because it isn't going to be communicated in words, it's going to be communicated in actions. It isn't going to be put into a picture frame, it's going to put into operation. Employees will remember it not because they see it on the walls around them every day, but because they see it in the behavior of everyone in the organization all around them every day. How managers talk about it won't matter so much; how *workers* talk about it will be what counts.

So how does the actual culture shift toward alignment along a goal like this one begin? What's the first step?

Well, in this case the first step actually has four steps.

The Four-Step Experiment

Time to play *Doctor's Dilemma*. Put yourself for a moment in the shoes of a dedicated doctor who has two seriously overweight patients. The doctor naturally hopes to improve the overall health of both, as any caring doctor would. The first patient's goal: to avoid diabetes, heart disease, and other illnesses associated with obesity. The doctor works with this patient to design a comprehensive diet and exercise regimen that will restore physical fitness—a regimen that among its other benefits will also produce a dramatic weight loss. The second patient's goal: to look more attractive in a bathing suit. (For the purposes of illustration, let's say this patient is driven by the cardinal sin of pride.) The doctor once again designs a fitness regimen, but this patient ultimately decides such an approach will take too much time and effort. So instead he decides to go on a crash starvation diet. Pounds do come off, but a variety of symptoms begin to appear that suggest resistance to disease is diminishing, and overall health is deteriorating. Also, unable to sustain the willpower to endure food deprivation day after day, the patient soon gives in to hunger cravings and packs the weight back on. Doctor's dilemma: how to convince this impatient patient that real and lasting weight loss can only be achieved as part of a broader program to improve overall health, rather than in a quickie effort to just shed pounds.

Now a similar case. A "doctor of organizational culture" has two businesses as patients, and hopes to help both improve their overall cultural health. The leadership team's goal in the first business: to improve employee morale, raise customer retention levels, and achieve better results overall. The doctor helps this patient implement a three-pronged alignment strategy like the one outlined in the chapters that follow. The leadership team's goal in the second business: make more money. (For the purposes of illustration, let's say this business is driven by the cardinal sin of greed.) The doctor once again outlines an alignment strategy, but this business favors what it considers a more direct route to the objective: it simply intensifies the pressure on everyone to do whatever it takes to improve the bottom line. Operating capacities are reduced to cut costs, workers are laid off, and already low employee morale sinks even lower. A brief rise in profits is followed by a leveling out at worse levels than ever before. Doctor's dilemma: how to convince this impatient patient that the goal of higher profits will be more effectively and permanently achieved as part of a broader program to improve organizational alignment, rather than in a quickie effort to just pump up the bottom line.

How *do* you convince someone that what appears to be a less direct way to the finish line will often turn out to be the quickest way (and sometimes even the only way) to reach it? It's a tough sell for both doctors—which of course is why there are still so many dangerously obese people around us, and why there are still so many dangerously unprofitable businesses around us.

One time-honored technique around this kind of dilemma is the "start small and build on successes" approach. The prescription: try the regimen on for size, on a test basis, on a small scale. See how it feels. If you like the results, repeat the dosage as necessary. That's the approach we're going to adopt in our four-step "experiment in culture shifting." We're going to attempt to create a powerful little pocket of motivational alignment in one small corner of your organizational culture. And we're going to use employee involvement and ownership as key catalysts. If the treatment works and seems relatively painless and free of undesirable side effects, then you can repeat as necessary.

The experiment's four steps are as follows:

1. Have One (or Several) Employee(s) Come Up with One (or Several) Idea(s) to Improve the Customer Experience

Depending on how large your employee population is, and how large a "motivational blip" you'd like to create on this first trial run, this experiment can work with a single employee's single idea, or with a batch of ideas from several members of a single work team. (I'll outline the following as if there's to be only a single idea involved, to avoid awkward constructions like "his/her/their idea(s)" or "implementing it/them." Please bear in mind throughout this section that references to a single idea could also be referring to more than one.) In theory, the idea could come out of a suggestion box or a questionnaire—but since *involvement* is just as important as *ownership* in this experiment, there's a far more engaging way to generate an appropriate idea.

The quantity—and more important, quality—of employees' ideas will always be higher when they're the product of a structured, facilitated, interactive process. Inviting workers to come up with a general blue-sky idea to improve the customer experience *overall* is in most cases simply too broad a blank canvas to work with. Telling a would-be artist, "You have 10 minutes—paint a beautiful scene" is not at all the same as saying, "You have 10 minutes—paint an apple dangling from a branch." To narrow the scope of the assignment to a more manageable scale, try setting up a little meeting in which the sole objective is to zero in on one aspect of the customer experience in particular—perhaps one that everyone acknowledges is often a source of frustration, for example—and invite ideas (through dialogue and give-and-take) to improve that one aspect.

As an illustration of how our four-step experiment might unfold, let's imagine that one Tuesday morning manager Chris brings the work team together for a brainstorming session and invites the participants to identify some sources of customer frustration in typical business transactions.

"Customers hate having to fill out all the paperwork," says one worker.

"They hate having to wait in line," says another.

"They hate it when the person serving them answers the phone and then ignores them while taking care of the other customer on the phone," says a third.

Manager Chris records all of these issues on a flip chart and then reviews each one in turn, inviting ideas for improving the situation in each case.

Worker Terry feels the "waiting in line" problem is especially hard on older customers, because Terry's own grandparents once complained at length about it at the dinner table. So Terry offers this idea: "We could put out a bench that's just for senior citizens to use while waiting. That way they don't lose their place in the line."

The rest of the team responds favorably to this idea, so Chris decides to make it the basis for the experiment. Chris first asks if this is something Terry would like to personally be involved in setting up. "Absolutely, definitely," says Terry. Step one is done; Chris now has an idea to work with.

2. Help the Employee Successfully Implement the Idea

In our example, "successful implementation" implies two separate developments.

First, an actual bench designated for seniors appears out on the floor. The employee who came up with the idea can hardly be expected to pay for this bench out-of-pocket, so "helping with the implementation" in this case will include incurring the cost of acquiring and installing the bench, and perhaps some signage designating the bench for seniors. It might also involve rearranging the floor plan slightly, to make allowances for the bench. Manager Chris should get Terry involved in as many of these decisions and activities as possible; helping with the implementation doesn't mean taking over and doing it all yourself. EIO: Employee involvement and ownership is key.

The second aspect of "successful implementation": seniors must genuinely perceive the bench as a positive change. No unforeseen disadvantages of providing a bench come to light. Nobody is inconvenienced by the presence of the bench.

If for whatever reason the bench turns out not to be a hit, the implementation was not successful. But note this important distinction: a failed implementation of a given idea does not mean the four-step experiment *itself* has failed. There is no experiment at all *unless* the idea is successfully implemented. To put it another way, this is not an experiment to see whether seniors might appreciate a bench; it's an experiment to see whether letting employees come up with their own strategies for delighting customers will create cultural alignment and drive up employee motivation. The only way to make this four-step experiment valid and meaningful is to ensure that customers are, in fact, delighted by the employees' ideas in step two, so that the experiment can then proceed to steps three and four. If step two's a bust, the experiment was never concluded.

3. Make It Easy and Convenient for Customers to Supply Positive Feedback About the Idea

If Step Two is accomplished, it means customers are happy about the change. But in many cases customers will tend to keep their happiness to themselves, at least until someone comes along and gives them an easy and comfortable opportunity to express it. In our example, for step three of the experiment manager Chris strikes up friendly, informal one-minute conversations with seniors sitting on the bench. Chris first asks for the customers' overall impressions of how the business is treating them. If nothing about the bench is forthcoming, Chris then solicits it directly: "I notice you're using the bench we recently installed, how's that working out for you …?" The object is to create opportunities for spontaneous expressions of appreciation and delight about the change to flow from the source. When that happens, Step Three is complete.

4. Use This Feedback As the Basis for Employee Recognition

A bench for seniors was Terry's idea. It would naturally be very gratifying for Terry to get a solid pat on the back from manager Chris for this innovation. But as mentioned in the Introduction, positive feedback from impartial *external* sources usually carries a much greater motivational impact. In our example, as the seniors are expounding on how they appreciate the thoughtfulness of the bench, and actually drive slightly out of their way to do business here (despite a competitor closer to home) precisely because of the bench, Chris takes notes. These remarks will later be incorporated into some kind of formal recognition and celebration for Terry. Even better: if circumstances permit, manager Chris points to Terry working nearby while telling the delighted customers, "This bench was actually Terry's idea," and promptly summons Terry over. "Sorry to interrupt you, Terry, but these folks would like to tell you something about your bench." The seniors rhapsodize to Terry about the bench, and Chris steps back and says nothing. Chris merely observes.

With the final step concluded, all that remains is to observe the effects of the experiment. Has this whole "bench for seniors" thing had a positive effect on Terry, overall? Does the employee seem proud of the idea, proud of the effect it's having on customers? Has it affected Terry's general "mood" or "attitude" about the job in any noticeable and lasting way? If there were to be more brainstorming to uncover ideas for delighting customers, would Terry be even more eager to participate? Would other employees too, perhaps, be more eager to come up with a winning idea of their own?

Profound Lessons from the Road Runner

It's normally not at all difficult to assess the results of this experiment.

If, for example, all four steps of the experiment were followed as outlined above, and this produced no discernible effect on the employee who came up with the idea, then it's fair to say the experiment failed. That is, you will have succeeded in improving the customer experience by adding a new source of delight for the customers involved—which is good news for any business—but this will not have contributed to a corresponding improvement in morale or motivation for the employees involved. You will still have gained something, even if slightly less than you were hoping for. (I have never personally witnessed this kind of result, but I'm willing to allow that it is at least theoretically possible.)

So what might have caused the experiment to (hypothetically) fail in such a case? Did the idea's complexity or cost outweigh the benefit it delivered to customers? Was the impact on customers too slight to generate powerful feedback? Did the employee feel management had taken over the implementation to such an extent that the sense of personal ownership for the idea had been lost? Did it feel to the employee that management was somehow taking credit for the idea, either with customers or with the senior leadership team? Any number of factors might be at play.

What's the best course of action when the four-step experiment (hypothetically) fails? If I were the doctor advising a patient with this problem, I'd immediately sit the patient down to watch a road runner cartoon.

The hero (?) of these classic cartoons is a hungry and resourceful coyote. The coyote's basic objective is clear and unchanging, and he even occasionally shares his strategic vision with us: a steaming roasted road runner on his dinner plate. Though the vision may be clear, however, the actual mission keeps changing. A typical mission might involve suspending an anvil from a hot air balloon, and using an electric fan to propel the rig along, and relying on a stick of dynamite with a long fuse to release the anvil once everything is nicely in position over the bird.

Despite a strong strategic objective, where this coyote tends to be weak is in the area of tactical implementation. In preparation for the launch of his hot air balloon, for example, the coyote lights the long fuse to the dynamite—and discovers to his dismay that the fuse burns along its entire length in less than a second and the dynamite blows up in his face. The coyote's blackened, charred figure walks dejectedly out of the frame. Fade out. Fade in: the coyote has conceived a whole new mission, using a large catapult and a massive boulder, etc.

Our coyote, already dangerously undernourished, is almost certainly going to starve to death. He has abandoned the whole anvil-and-balloon mission because of a defective dynamite fuse. He will subsequently abandon the whole catapult-and-boulder mission because of a defective spring mechanism in the catapult. The coyote has come up with dozens, if not *hundreds*, of separate, ingenious schemes by which to catch the road runner—any one of which might have been made to work with a little tweaking. But this coyote is in far too big a hurry to sit down and review existing tactical schemes, and refine them. Like most of the people in the audience, laughing as they identify with his methods and predicaments, he would much rather scrap one experiment at the first sign of failure and move on to another. And, like many in the audience, he consistently finds himself dealing with disappointment.

My counsel to the coyote: stick with any one of your tactical schemes long enough to really *see it through*. In the case of the anvil idea, for example, ask yourself, what would the optimal fuse-burning time be? Does it need to be dynamite at all—what about some sort of remote-control anvil-release mechanism you could activate yourself at the optimal moment? Create a checklist: what are all the things that could blow up in your face, pound you into the ground, flatten you like an accordion, or cause you to fall from a great height with an accompanying whistling sound that descends in pitch as you plummet toward the canyon floor—and how will you prevent these from happening? Refine each of the various elements, anticipate and work out the bugs. *Make it work*. Your very survival may depend on it.

If the four-step experiment failed, I would say have at least one more go at it. In our example, is the bench in the best location? Is the signage clear? Refine the elements, work out the bugs. *Make it work*. Your very survival may depend on it.

Let The Culture-Shift Begin

Far more typically, the four-step experiment will have an unmistakably positive effect on the employees involved. Virtually no one is immune to the motivational effect of encouragement, of appreciation, of positive feedback for their work and their efforts—and this, again, is especially true when it originates from impartial sources.

"I'm not exaggerating," says Beth Guastella of the Kate Spade chain of stores, "I bet there are at least either two e-mails and/or hard notes that we get per week where a customer has taken the time to write about a particular associate experience.... When I call the stores, when I visit the stores, you can see it, you can see it on their faces ... you just see a lot of smiles, you hear the smiles on the phone ... and certainly the managers articulate [this] far better than I, but, let's call it an additional spring in their step when they [arrive] in the morning. They're very happy to be there."[9]

Camille Maxwell is Office Coordinator at the Parks & Resorts division of Delaware North Companies (DNC). "When you get immediate, immediate recognition," she says, "honestly, I just have to say, it keeps your spirits up about being where you're located, in your position. It just brings out that energy: 'I love my job, I like what I do, I want to advance.'"[10]

"When an employee sees their idea that's being used and they see it happening, it brings about a pride," says Paula Davis, in charge of training in the Quality Network Suggestion Program at General Motors, and a past president of the Employee Involvement Association. "Everybody wants to be recognized."[11]

In big companies or small, in retail or manufacturing or you-name-it—positive recognition for the workers' own ideas and efforts is the universal constant, the supreme motivator of them all.

The four-step experiment is an easy and persuasive way to convince skeptics that:

- It's not only possible, but *preferable*, to improve employee motivation and customer satisfaction as part of a single strategic initiative.
- Inviting employees to come up with their own solutions to sources of customer dissatisfaction introduces an element of play-like challenge into the workplace.

- Increasing the levels of employee involvement and ownership intensifies the motivational effect of positive feedback and recognition.
- Direct positive feedback and recognition from an external source carries greater and longer-lasting motivational impact than from an internal source.
- It's not only possible, but *preferable*, to transform an entire organizational culture by starting small and letting the enthusiasm spread at its own unforced pace.

In our example, what should manager Chris do next, after seeing the motivational effect the customers' feedback had on Terry? Well, there were two additional customer irritants that emerged in the original brainstorming meeting: the amount of paperwork required, and the tendency to give phone-in customers priority over those on the premises. How about giving one or more of the other workers a chance to experience what Terry did? How about enhancing the customer experience with a few more creative solutions from other workers, to generate some more spontaneous positive feedback? In short, how about turning the one-of-a-kind four-step experiment into an *ongoing four-step process*?

This is how a cultural transformation can be set in motion in any organization. Individual workers, like individual iron filings, are brought into alignment through a tiny shift of attitude or position, until the entire overall pattern of the culture is visibly and dramatically different. Start small, and build on successes.

The question then becomes, once the genie's out of the bottle and the magic has begun, how do we avoid the various pitfalls and ensure everything's progressing toward the kind of flashpoint effect we're aspiring to?

That's the subject matter in the remaining chapters of this book.

Notes

1. Cheryl Beall, *Retail 101*, interview with the author, October 20, 2006.
2. For more on the power of aspirational fields to create alignment in work and in life, see Paul Levesque and Art McNeil, *Dreamcrafting:*

The Art of Dreaming Big, The Science of Making It Happen (San Francisco, CA: Berrett-Koehler, 2003).

3. Brian Gallagher, Lindt & Sprüngli, interview with the author, November 15, 2006.
4. Ibid.
5. Cheryl Beall interview.
6. Brian Gallagher interview.
7. Beth Guastella, Kate Spade stores, interview with the author, November 10, 2006.
8, Stewart Collins, DNC, interview with the author, November 3, 2006.
9. Beth Guastella interview.
10. Camille Maxwell, DNC, interview with the author, Oct. 31, 2006.
11. Paula Davis, General Motors, interview with the author, December 4, 2006.

Chapter 4

A New Role for Internal Communication

Anyone who's ever been responsible for putting out an employee newsletter will know how challenging it can be to generate content the staff will find interesting and relevant. (I speak from personal experience, as the long-ago editor of a corporate newsletter for a large digital telecommunications company.) While top management wants a big splashy feature in the newsletter on how technical improvements in the new Transplexer products promise to generate significant revenues in the next quarter, the employees themselves tend to be far more interested in the photos of Tammy's new twin boys and the company softball game.

"I have been consistently shocked at how important [internal communication] actually is to employees," says retail consultant Cheryl Beall, "how much they honestly really care about it. Some kind of a mention in the employee newsletter, and they're like diving down the hall to get it. And I have to admit, it really quite frankly shocks me."[1]

Even farther back in my own previous work life, I was for a number of years involved in the control-room production of daily newscasts in a TV station serving a large local audience. I learned a great deal about how news information is most effectively "packaged" to attract and hold viewers. To this day, in your community and mine, the national networks' evening news programs are typically followed (or preceded) by a local news program. Both broadcasts originate in very similar studio production facilities, using very similar kinds of cameras and microphones and lighting equipment. Where the network program will focus on the major national and global calamities of the day, the local program will often consist of stories about police summoned to break up a noisy late-night party on Elm Road, and a kitten rescued from a storm drain on Maple Drive. Not always the most gripping fare—so what is it about these local newscasts that keeps the audience coming back for more? There's inevitably some excitement in the voice of a viewer who cries, "Hey, I know where that is—that's right near where I live!" The excitement is even greater when the viewer can cry, "Hey, I know that guy! I went to school with that guy!" The biggest excitement of all, of course, is when the cry becomes, "Hey, that's *me* right there, on the left!" As with the employee newsletter, it can be exciting—it can be *motivating*—to see something of ourselves in or on "the news"—or in any form of positive media exposure that our friends and relatives know is being seen by lots of other people as well.

Most businesses have at least a vague understanding of how this particular form of excitement works, but even in these settings it can sometimes be surprising to observe workers "diving down the hall" to get their hands on a newsletter in which they are mentioned. The motivational power of this kind of internal communication has typically been greatly underappreciated (and therefore underutilized)—a situation we shall herein endeavor to correct.

The Medium Is the Message

Let's discuss basics for a moment. In any business setting, what function does internal communication serve, at the most basic level? It doesn't matter if the mechanism is an employee newsletter (in print or electronic format), an employee bulletin board, regularly scheduled staff meetings, general distribution e-mails or memos, or any combination of these and others besides—what would you say is the primary objective of these things in your own organization?

When I've casually asked this question of managers over the years, they've mostly tended to treat the answer as simple and obvious: these tools exist for the purpose of imparting *information* of various kinds. These are information tools for our information age. Their job is to keep people within the organization up-to-date, in-the-know. And if as a secondary benefit they also happen to contribute in some way to a sense of pride or team spirit, well then, hey, all the better.

Simple and obvious as this may seem, it's not quite the basic function of internal communication in *all* organizations. In those that operate within a flashpoint culture (that is, one in which employee motivation and customer satisfaction fuel each other in closed loop of contagious enthusiasm), the primary role of internal communication is to *reinforce cultural alignment.*

This is a significantly different objective. It changes the kind of information that will be conveyed, and it changes the way it will be conveyed. The emphasis, at all times, is to show employees a reflection of themselves caught in the act of being "useful and necessary in the world" (or at the very least, being useful and necessary in the organization). These are not called *employee* newsletters and *employee* bulletin boards and *employee* meetings for nothing. The information conveyed through these mechanisms is solely, exclusively, for the edification of employees—as opposed to the *education* of employees (for the edification of management).

In flashpoint businesses, the company newsletter is *not* where management announces new strategic initiatives for the business—not even initiatives that directly affect the workers. Management uses other mechanisms to report on management activity, as the situation warrants. Those pipelines of internal communication that operate on a continual and regular basis are devoted solely to the intensification of cultural alignment at the employee level. And this is achieved primarily by putting as many employees "in the news" as can be squeezed into the available space. *Everybody* goes diving down the hall to get their hands on the latest newsletter in this kind of business, because the content is exclusively hero stories of one kind or another about *them*. In cultural terms, the communication media themselves become the message—by the nature of their content, they become transformed from a *reflection* of alignment into a *source* of alignment.

An unforgettable example from personal experience: years ago, in a client organization in Ottawa, Canada, a custodial employee had come up with an ingenious way to eliminate a slip hazard for customers approaching the building on wet or snowy days. A story about it, with a photo of the employee, was featured in the company newsletter. But it was customary for this organization to mail copies of its newsletter to the *children* of any employees highlighted within its pages, with a personalized note advising the kids that, "Your daddy's picture appears on page 2." Several weeks later, this employee was at an all-hands meeting in which management was inviting questions or comments about the company's quality improvement program. The custodian rose to his feet to speak, which immediately struck many of those around him as unusual. (This worker was seen as a crusty old veteran of the company who tended to pretty much keep to himself.) He proceeded to report that the day his two children received the newsletter, he'd been greeted with a hero's welcome when he got home. The youngsters wanted to hear all about how his picture came to be in "the paper." His kids had subsequently brought the newsletter to school for show-and-tell, and the teacher had posted it on the school bulletin board for a week. The kids felt like celebrities at school, he said, as if their dad had been on the cover of *Time* magazine. He went on to acknowledge, in a more sub-dued tone of voice, that he had always assumed his children were some-what ashamed of the janitorial work their father did for a living. This expression of pride from his own kids, he said, was the most personally rewarding experience in his entire 30-year career—and if this was the kind of thing the company meant by "quality improvement," he wanted the managers to know he was ready to do anything he could to help. With that, he sat back down. Things were strangely quiet in that meeting room for a few moments after his remarks.

Killing Two Paradoxes with One Stone

Is the foregoing intended to suggest that simply stuffing the newsletter (or other internal communication media) with more photos of employees and more stories about employees will automatically intensify alignment?

If only it were that easy. Doing so may make these communication media more intrinsically *interesting* to employees, which of course is a good thing in itself. But to intensify cultural alignment requires more than a change of content. It requires a context—a unifying *theme*—to which all of this content must be clearly linked. To put it another way, there can be no alignment until there exists a powerful aspirational field to become aligned to in the first place.

The idea of an aspirational *theme* for everything that takes place every day across the organization is one of the greatest lessons we can learn from flashpoint businesses. This theme is more than a mission or a vision or a set of values. These may change with time, to reflect changes in the mar-ketplace or in the organization itself—whereas the context is the cultural piece that *never* changes. Some businesses actually give their aspirational theme a name and brand identity of its own. (At Delaware North Companies, for example, it's called *GuestPath*. It's an example we'll be tak-ing a close look at shortly.) What's especially revealing is that most of these businesses typically did not use their existing internal communication media to "announce" or "launch" their cultural theme at its inception. If there was ever an official announcement from on high about it, this was kept entirely apart from the traditional internal communication channels and was treated as a special one-time event. More often there was no formal announcement or official launch *at all*.

This certainly cuts against the grain of conventional management practice. Bring a typical group of managers together for a planning meeting, get them excited about a "new strategic direction" for their business, and almost without fail the first and most pressing question they tackle is, "How are we going to communicate this to the rest of the organization?" Much of the wind comes out of their sails as they contemplate the cynicism and resistance they'll immediately encounter from their skeptical workforce. All their creative energies shift from contemplation of an exciting new direction to contemplation of a familiar old problem—how on earth are they going to convince everybody that this time it's different, this time they really are determined to make it happen? Just wrestling with the problem is sometimes discouraging enough to undermine their own confidence in the achievability of their new plan.

In Chapter 2 reference was made to the "profit paradox" (to wit, those businesses that are most profitable are often the ones that do *not* make the pursuit of profit their number-one priority). There's a solution for communication challenges like the one described above, but it means coming to grips with two more paradoxes.

First Communication Paradox: Everybody complains that they're swamped with too many reports and memos and documents and information in general—yet everybody feels "we never know what's going on around here," and "nobody ever tells us anything."

When Brian Gallagher of Lindt & Sprüngli discusses his experience with employee surveys, "... and I've gone through this in many organizations," he's quick to point out, "the one thing that always stands out [is] employees always want more communication. If nothing, it makes us realize each time we do this how important it is to get the communication piece better every chance we get."[2]

But how do you improve things when the same people who want more seemingly also want less? Some might interpret the paradox to mean workers feel they're getting too much *irrelevant* information combined with not enough *relevant* information. This sounds plausible enough, but on closer inspection, wouldn't an abundance of reports and memos and documents and information in general almost *by default* paint a composite picture of "what's going on around here" (whether the recipient happens to like what's going on around here or not)? Isn't this precisely the kind of "relevant" information these recipients claim to be lacking?

In most cases, this feeling of forever being in the dark about where the business is headed is *not* caused by relevant information being withheld. It's caused by another problem altogether, a far more basic (and more serious) problem—namely, that the business is *not headed anywhere.* It's the classic manifestation of lack of alignment—everybody's pulling or being pulled in a different direction. Employees who gripe about being kept in the dark are often giving their management team the benefit of the doubt; they're assuming management is leading the business somewhere and for some vague selfish reason is simply choosing to withhold the details. In reality, management's collective failing is a lot scarier than that. Theirs is a ship sailing choppy waters with no bearing whatsoever, where the only real "mission" is to somehow remain afloat for as long as possible.

In businesses that adopt an aspirational theme for organization-wide alignment, the first communication paradox is usually resolved as if by magic. No one is unclear, any more, about where this business is going and how it intends to get there.

Second Communication Paradox: Everybody resists change—yet everybody says they're dissatisfied with the *status quo.*

Once again, at first glance, this sounds likes like a clear contradiction. Some might interpret this one to mean "we may be tired of the way things are around here, but please don't do anything to make things *worse.*" Yet seasoned organizational change agents know from direct personal experience that employees will often resist even changes intended only to make things better for them—including things as seemingly positive as a basic raise in pay (as Cheryl Beall related in Chapter 2). In World War II, when the allied forces first discovered the Nazi death camps and threw open the gates, many of the surviving inmates were so emotionally battered they at first seemed strangely reluctant to leave.

I'll let the anthropologists decide whether resistance to change represents a hard-wired evolutionary adaptation for survival in humans. For our purposes, it's enough to acknowledge that virtually all change meets with at least some resistance—and that in business cultures where workers have long felt unfairly treated by management, even dramatic changes for the better will typically meet with *considerable* resistance, especially when first announced.

In those flashpoint businesses where the aspirational theme for change is not directly announced or formally "launched" at all, this second communication paradox is resolved in a subtle but very effective way. In simple terms, the change is allowed to "sneak up" on the affected employees *one benefit at a time*. They're allowed to experience the individual positive results of the change even before they have a chance to muster up much in the way of negative resistance to it. Bit by bit, the tired "old way" of doing things is replaced by a more engaging and motivational "new way," all the while bypassing the resistance phase that would otherwise normally accompany—and hinder—any such cultural change effort.

Is this an underhanded, manipulative way to handle things? No more than "plotting" to surprise a loved one with a secret gift or birthday party. In both cases, some aspects of the preparation may be concealed—and in both cases, the purpose of this "deception" is purely to heighten the pleasure and enjoyment the recipient will derive from the experience.

But how do we go about making a new organization-wide aspirational theme "sneak up" on workers one benefit at a time, especially when our ultimate objective is to create cultural alignment? A diagram may help explain how the process unfolds.

The Culture Map

Imagine if there was a way to map out an organizational culture on paper.

For the sake of illustration, we'll use this diagram to represent the existing culture in a hypothetical business organization.

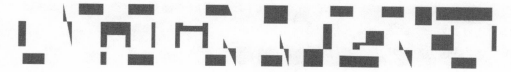

In this map, each shape represents a particular element of the organization's culture. Let's say that the longer horizontal rectangle in the upper right, for example, represents management's performance appraisal process. Another shape nearby is the existing employee recognition program. All the various processes, policies, and procedures that govern the operation are each represented by an individual shape in the map. In its entirety, this layout represents the cultural "landscape" of the organization. It may look like a meaningless jumble of elements—but as workers get used to the way the business operates, they learn to navigate their way through this landscape, avoiding obstacles and roadblocks, creating shortest-route pathways between key points, etc. In short, the contours of the terrain may strike them as somewhat meaningless, but at least they also become *familiar*.

Now let's say that over a given period of time, management introduces a few new elements here and there (represented by the darker shapes.)

The workers are aware that their landscape has changed a little, of course, but the *overall pattern* of the layout still looks familiar to them. These changes are not significant enough to trigger major alarms; they're the kind of little changes most people expect to have to deal with over time. More important, in a variety of ways some of these changes have actually *improved* things for the workers. Nobody makes a fuss about it one way or the other, but the unspoken consensus among most employees is that these minor changes have either had no effect, or have had a beneficial effect. It doesn't take long for the workforce to become familiar and comfortable with this slightly modified cultural layout. The newer, darker shapes assume the paler color of "the familiar."

As time passes, additional little changes to the cultural landscape materialize (again represented by darker shapes).

Although the *overall pattern* continues to remain reassuringly familiar, by this point some of the employees, at least, are beginning to discern some meaning to what had always previously seemed a relatively random jumble of cultural elements. Their organization's culture, as a whole, seems to be starting to "say something." As before, these most recent changes have produced no adverse effects, and in some cases quite significant positive effects. Whether as a result of the changes or not, working in this environment has consistently become more satisfying and rewarding over time. The workers quickly become familiar with this slightly modified layout. It doesn't take long for these newer darker shapes to assume the paler tone of familiar elements.

Minor changes to the cultural landscape continue to appear at regular intervals (once more represented by the darker shapes).

Despite little change to the familiar *overall pattern*, the sense of alignment in the cultural landscape has by this point become clear to virtually everyone who works there. There is now a clear and logical reason for all the shapes, and for their respective position and relationship to all the other shapes. All the cultural elements work in combination to support *one single idea*—an idea that's clear to all. And whether as a result of this, or as a happy coincidence, working in this culture has become more satisfying than ever.

Eventually, new cultural elements begin appearing less frequently, and the overall culture "settles in" to its more-or-less final form, with all elements taking on the same color of familiarity.

Now imagine that once this point is reached, those employees who were present for the entire cultural evolution are asked to recall the specific moment in time when "alignment" was actually achieved in their culture. How would they respond? Many might be inclined to say "we've had alignment from the very beginning," since a great deal of their cultural landscape *does*, in fact, date back to the beginning. (If you look back at the first culture map, above, you too may observe that all the "makings" of alignment were already in place, even if they weren't recognizable as such at first.) And even among those employees who can recall a time when theirs was a far less satisfying environment to work in, they'll be unable to agree on one particular moment when alignment suddenly took hold. It just kind of snuck up on them.

This is cultural change by evolution, rather than by revolution. Huge (and in some cases, impenetrable) walls of employee resistance can sometimes be avoided altogether, simply by resisting the temptation to formally announce the culture-change initiative at its inception. Or to restate it in even simpler terms: sometimes it's better to *show* 'em how you're going to make things better, rather than *tell* 'em. The telling often does nothing more than create widespread anxiety, and it gives cynics and resistors plenty of time to dig in their heels and dream up ways to negate or undermine the change.

To our management group in their planning room, whose enthusiasm for their new strategic direction is eroding as they wrestle with how to formally *announce* the change, I would propose skipping the announcement altogether. Just start introducing the change bit by bit, and let your employees discover the related benefits one at a time. In fact, the primary function for your existing internal communication channels should become to *highlight* those benefits. Especially if your new aspirational theme gives workers on-the-job opportunities to feel "useful and necessary in the world," the role of internal communication becomes to publicize hero stories of workers doing useful and necessary things for customers in particular, or for the community at large. Internal communication becomes a key mechanism to illustrate the positive effects of alignment—and this is how it also becomes a motivational tool that actually *intensifies* alignment.

From Teamwork to Themework

For the leadership team at Houston-based Stage Stores, the issue was customer service. At the time of this writing, there are over 650 stores across 33 states in the Stage Stores retail chain, under such brands as Palais Royal, Peebles, and Bealls (no relation to Cheryl Beall). "At this time we do about $1.2 billion a year," says VP of Store Operations Mark Emmitte, who's been with Stage for over 20 years. "This year [2006], in fact, in the Peebles division alone, we grew by about a hundred stores."3

Despite their success, the executives at Stage Stores felt their customer service levels were falling short, and the team was eager to correct the situation. They considered a number of approaches but ultimately liked the emphasis on employee involvement and ownership in the book *Customer Service Made Easy*. They invited its author to lead them through a planning session for creating a new, more customer-focused culture across the organization.

The planning session "was really profound for us," says Mark Emmitte. "Having spent most of my career in training and development, I've had a tendency to be somewhat skeptical of other training and development efforts, simply because I've read all the books, I've heard it all before, I've trained most of it before myself. And I will tell you very honestly that I completely changed my point of view. We're just so excited about it. We're really diving into this, that is how much an impact it's had on us. It's been tremendous. We're just really pleased with the progress we've made so far."4

The progress Mark refers to is the executive team's decision to begin applying without delay the four-step process outlined in the previous chapter. "We started out immediately following the [planning] session that we had here [by bringing together] our field manager crew," he explains. In keeping with the employee-involvement-and-ownership approach, the executives bypassed a formal "announcement" that a major culture change was coming and instead proceeded directly to a second planning day. This time, however, some 70 Stage Store managers were the participants, "... so they understand the importance of getting associates engaged, and seeking out and soliciting [associates' ideas to improve the customer experience]," as Mark explains.

This kind of collective brainstorming at the store-manager level was something new in the Stage Stores culture—a new "dark shape" appearing without much advance explanation on their culture map, so to speak. Did this one single session contribute in any significant way to a sense of alignment?

"Yes," says Mark, "and I can give you just an incredible example. Since [the session] included both district managers and loss prevention managers, very often you could have two very opposite views, because on the loss prevention side, controlling assets and preventing losses is their number one priority." (This is precisely the kind of "priority clash" that so often characterizes organizations lacking alignment.) Mark went on to describe one such loss-control mechanism in particular: "We have a program in place, and many banks use it, some other retailers use it, it's used when a customer writes a check—the customer is asked to put a thumbprint on the check. And the protection really is to apprehend someone in case of fraud, or identity theft.

"And what was so powerful to me is one of our loss prevention managers stood up [during the session] and was talking about [this control] and emphatically said, '*Why on earth are we doing this*, because it is completely contradictory to what we're saying here.' And I think what was very powerful is that they recognized it. Do we have to have controls in place? Absolutely, because we're still a business. Nevertheless, given ... the potential negative impact, we had to make a decision. Is the return we're getting on this big enough to offset the potential negative and adverse impact on customers? There is not only discussion about eliminating [that particular control], we have already eliminated it from three of our districts, and potentially will do it company-wide. What came out of that was, we absolutely have to have controls in place, but we have to have controls in place that accomplish business objectives *and* don't alienate our customers."[5]

You can almost see the word "alignment" beginning to take shape on their culture map.

Mark uses one word to describe the session: "Eye-opening. I think I can speak for all my colleagues here ... what we learned is that so many people have so many ideas—the real secret is getting those ideas to bubble to the surface. And out of sometimes [what may appear to be] crazy ideas, what ends up happening is then you end up coming up with something completely new, a fresh approach, and it just gets people involved and interested in what you're doing."

As he elaborates on what came out of this one session, it becomes increasingly apparent that he is speaking in terms of a new *context*—a theme—for the way the whole organization will operate. "It is completely changing the way [we] think," he admits. "If every single thing we do is not focused on it, it is so easy to slip up and do something that is detrimental to the effort. Everything we do has to say we're committed to our customers, and equally important, to our associates—and that we do care what people think and what they have to say, and that good ideas come from lots of different places."[6]

Mark and his colleagues know their transition to a fully aligned culture is still only in the early stages. "We are not going to change overnight," he acknowledges. "But when you brainstorm, that's what's so invaluable about [it], the ideas come out of that, [and] eventually you get there. You find a way."

At Stage Stores, the "communication strategy" was to show managers, not tell them, how the new approach was going to work and what it was going to feel like. At the time of this writing, these managers had not yet brought the first step of the four-step process (*"Have employees come up with their own ideas to improve the customer experience"*) down to the worker-bee level. Their intention is to do so using the Novations *Customer Service from the Inside Out* program, which translates the four-step process into a series of structured employee brainstorming sessions internal trainers can facilitate with various work teams. But the first order of business was to get the support of the managers themselves for this approach. Allowing them to experience it firsthand proved a simpler and far more effective way to get buy-in than attempting to describe it in memos or newsletters or formal presentations by senior management.

Similarly, in the previous chapter Beth Guastella (senior VP of retail at Kate Spade) described her "roadmap" exercise, in which her employees take the lead in defining the next year's business priorities. Here again, the familiar "internal communication of new strategies creates resistance" cycle is bypassed by proceeding directly to employee involvement and ownership. As Beth explains, this works far better "... than me just kind of creating this calendar and 'here's all the things we have coming up, here are the tasks that are going to have to be completed, here are the big projects that are on the horizon,' etc. etc. It's not just, to use Pete's words [Peter Ambrozaitis of Novations], it's not a 'tell-direct' type of environment. It's very participatory."[7]

Organizational alignment is the sense that "we're all pulling in the same direction." This "same direction" is the *theme* for everything that takes place in every corner of the organization every day. The role of internal communication is not to declare or define this direction (which invites resistance), but rather to demonstrate how it is being lived, to report on successes, to make heroes of those who are leading the way (which invites participation). Some businesses are better at doing this than others. We're about to learn from one of the best.

Brand Recognition

In World War II the generals planning the allied invasion of Nazi-occupied Europe via the Normandy beaches referred to the mission by its code name, *Operation Overlord*. Today most people use another name for that invasion: D-Day. The phrase "D-Day" was at the time a generic way of designating any "target date"—such-and-such an event was scheduled for "H-Hour on D-Day." But "D-Day" quickly became the name by which the allied invasion of Normandy in particular was known, and today the phrase is almost never used to refer to anything else. Similarly, "ground zero" once meant the exact location of any particular explosion or catastrophe, but in recent years it has come to refer to the site of the terrorist attacks on the World Trade Center in New York. This event was described by journalists at the time as "the September eleventh attacks" but today is more widely referred to simply as *Nine-Eleven*. When filmmakers or graphic artists create posters that refer to the attacks by placing a numeral "nine" to the left of two vertical blocks that resemble the twin towers but act as two "ones," they are in effect creating a logo—a visual symbol, or "brand"—for this world-shaking event.

Companies know the value of their corporate logos and go to considerable pains to protect their logos and trademarks against misuse and legal infringement. They also know the value of giving their products catchy brand names. Is CARISSMA a new shampoo-conditioner, a new high-perform-ance car, a new line of high-fashion formal wear—or did I just make it up to illustrate a point?

Advertising agencies know that logos and brand names are *forms of com-munication*. They know that a light, delicate, florid logo, for example, com-municates a very different message about a business than does a blockish, thick, heavy logo. A restaurant called *Spike's* communicates by its very name that the bill of fare is going to be strikingly different from what you'll find at *Reginald's*.

Visitors touring the offices of Delaware North Companies will see the com-pany logo (a stylized representation of the letters DNC) in the kinds of places corporate logos typically appear. But they may see another, different, logo in an even wider range of places. It's the *GuestPath* logo, sometimes accompanied by its tagline, *Creating special experiences one guest at a time*. To cite only a few examples, the *GuestPath* logo crops up on expensive wine glasses, on special thank-you stationery, and, as at a staff Christmas party, even in the form of temporary tattoos (which most employees were happy to apply to their hands, but the more playful preferred to showcase directly on their faces).

But what exactly is *GuestPath*? In the simplest terms, says DNC's Stewart Collins, it's "a process about standards, about guest service, and those things that would contribute to a positive guest experience. If you start to think about the volume of guests, people that we [at DNC] touch, it's astronomical. We're in the operation of the three biggest national parks in the country. We're in 40 to 50 airports, we're in 40 to 50 sporting arenas. Chicago stadium alone is 60 thousand guests on a Sunday for a football game. What the program is about is providing an experience to each guest as if they're individuals, and you take that moment to connect with them on that one-on-one basis. Before *GuestPath* we knew that the guests were important, we knew that excellent guest service was important, but we didn't have that 'one-to-one relationship thing' in our culture. And so we were thinking about, okay, on any given Saturday in Yosemite National Park there's going to be 15 thousand, 20 thousand guests that come through, and we're going to process them. So we really spent a great deal of time organically growing and figuring this program out. Between four and five years ago was the formal start."

As he elaborates on the program's objectives, the topic of employee involvement and ownership soon enters the discussion. "I believe that it's based in the connection that the employee/associate has with what they touch. And in our case, we touch guests. And if they can make that personal connection, then they tend to feel that they have some ownership over the results. In our case there's a connection with those guests, and if I can help [a particular guest] go someplace and have a great time, well just vicariously, I'm kind of with them and I had a good time too. I've talked to many associates who feel that way.... When they were able to, at the end of the day, say, 'Wow, I remember, that family came in and they were all nervous about what their experience as going to be, they'd saved up, driven from Iowa, it was this once-in-a-lifetime kind of thing, and there was so much pressure that it was going to be great—and by me being able to be involved with that, they had a great time, and I was involved with it so that really it's important to me.' And there's lots of, lots of examples I can give for that."

As I discuss the *GuestPath* program with Stewart Collins, I can hardly fail to notice that the program logo appears prominently on the vest he is wearing. And when he hands me his business card, there's the DNC logo beneath his name, as you'd expect—but on the reverse side, in dead center, is the GuestPath logo.

"You know the logo is very deliberate," he says. "It depicts a person stepping through a circle ... and they're carrying this single star that represents excellence." The connotation is someone jumping through a hoop. "Exactly," Stewart smiles, "to provide that great service."

At DNC, *GuestPath* is the all-encompassing context for organizational alignment. But in this company the context has been given a name. And more than a name: a full-blown brand identity. The program's aspirational theme is spelled out in the tagline, in simple straightforward language everyone can understand. That theme is what this company stands for. There's no mistaking what this company is about.

"In order to keep a staff motivated," Stewart says, "they really need to know that everybody is pointed in the same direction. 'Path' has a connotation of a direction, and it was very deliberate. So I think that helps to solidify the common goal. So if ... they have a common goal, and they're working with common interests, it's fairly easy, I think, to keep people motivated to excel at their role within that organization. ... You have to keep the staff busy, motivated, challenged, and that helps them feel that they have contributed to this great organization."

Stewart describes how the program has expanded over the years to encompass almost every aspect of the company's culture. "We have our Universal Service Standards," he says, "we have our Operating Standards, we have a Continuous Improvement Cycle that we do with the standards, [we deliver] training to the standards, [we focus on] measuring, rewarding, closing the gap." The logo on the reverse side of his business card is accompanied by the words *GuestPath Rewards!* Prior to the program's inception, he admits, "We had a very hit-or-miss consistency in rewarding, we weren't terribly good at it. We're really good at measuring things, [but] not terribly good at rewarding things, and we've really worked to bring that into part of the culture, to reward that excellence."

One of the greatest cultural benefits that derive from giving the theme for alignment such a prominent name and visual identity is that the basic role of all internal communication becomes unified along this same alignment axis. It will no longer be so challenging for the editor of the employee newsletter, for example, to come up with relevant and interesting content. Everything will revolve around *GuestPath* in one way or another. Letting senior managers experience firsthand the kinds of jobs frontline workers do for a day—that's called "Walking the GuestPath." Identifying and removing cultural obstacles to customer satisfaction—that becomes "Clearing the GuestPath." The program gives everyone a common language to describe all activities related to achieving their common goal. By spelling out the theme, the program's tagline (*Creating special experiences one guest at a time*) highlights the precise motive that motivates the whole organization. In this kind of setting, there's no need for what Brian Gallagher at Lindt Chocolate called the "complicated discussion" that arises "any time you have to talk about what it is you're trying to accomplish in a business." This is the better alternative to communicating a so-called mission statement in a frame on the wall. The aspirational theme itself becomes the supreme form of internal communication. It communicates to every employee every day a clear reminder of how their own individual contribution fits into the larger organizational objective. Newsletters and bulletin boards and memos and all other forms of internal communication become support mechanisms, with a common goal of their own—to reinforce the cultural alignment by reporting on its successes and champions.

Does this mean you should be thinking about assigning a name to the aspirational theme in your business? My answer: absolutely. I've had the experience of witnessing firsthand how energizing it can be to create this kind of "brand name" for what an organization is trying to accomplish. Years ago, for example, I was working with Raytheon Corporate Jets in the U.K. Their official corporate mission at that time incorporated three separate objectives: "guaranteed delivery performance" (the aircraft is always ready when promised), "a customer-friendly facility," and "the highest technical capability." They'd developed a customer feedback questionnaire that assigned a 1-to-10 rating scale to each of these three critical elements. Their theme for alignment thus became a numerical goal for the ratings they hoped to achieve: *10/10/10*.

In another British organization, the David Lloyd Leisure chain of fitness clubs, the alignment theme was christened *Heartbeat 135*. This number represents a healthy heart rate for most people, and the organization's mission at that time involved increasing their membership numbers to 135,000 by a particular date. The "heartbeat" theme also reflected their charitable partnership with the British Heart Foundation, so *Heartbeat 135* was meaningful to everyone in the organization.

Think you or your team might find it difficult to come up with a name for the aspirational theme in your business? My experience suggests it's easier than most people expect it to be. And if you're really stuck, you can always go with a semi-generic name like *The [Your Company Name] Challenge,* or *Operation [Your Company Name]*, or one of those made-to-order acronyms where each letter stands for a corporate value or idea.

The name itself is actually less important than what the theme communicates, simply by existing. Its message is unmistakable: this is what really matters around here. This is the reason behind everything that goes on in this place. The new role of internal communication is to continuously report on how the theme affects everything, links to everything, is the context for everything.

An aspirational theme, supported by internal communication, serves to focus the energies of all workers toward a single common objective. It's a simple mechanism, but it can produce profound change. A magnifying glass is a simple mechanism too—but by focusing the sun's rays down to a single point, it can start a fire that will completely transform the environment.

We describe flashpoint businesses as being "customer-focused." When collective energy is focused, a fire can be ignited in people's bellies. It's the first step toward triggering a flashpoint of contagious enthusiasm. All that remains is to use positive customer feedback as a key motivator to further intensify worker focus.

That's where *our* focus turns next.

Notes

1. Cheryl Beall, Retail 101, interview with the author, October 20, 2006.
2. Brian Gallagher, Lindt & Sprüngli, interview with the author, November 15, 2006.

3. Mark Emmitte, Stage Stores, interview with the author, December 5, 2006.
4. Ibid.
5. Ibid.
6. Ibid.
7. Beth Guastella, Kate Spade stores, interview with the author, November 10, 2006.

| Chapter 5 | # Customer Feedback and How to Get It |

The above images are photos I took of real signs on display in real places of business. Maybe signs like these are meant to be taken as a joke. Maybe not. Maybe half-and-half—you decide. Either way, though, messages like these (and many more that I've compiled over the years) can never be dismissed as "harmless." If I were writing another book on customer service, I'd offer these as tragic examples of businesses almost deliberately setting out to alienate their customers. But the subject of this book runs deeper, in terms of cultural dynamics within business settings. When we understand the power of a shared aspirational goal to focus energy and turn cynicism into enthusiasm, we recognize that these messages are doing even more harm than "just" alienating customers. They also represent tragic examples of businesses almost deliberately setting out to *demotivate their employees*. The sneering cynicism inherent in these messages (even if delivered with an implied wink) proclaims loud and clear to all employees that around here, a cynical attitude about customers is *okay*, it's justified, even we at the top of the organization feel the same way. Highly demotivating. Why should I as a worker even *try* to satisfy customers for whom the bosses themselves openly display such obvious contempt?

This chapter will discuss raising levels of customer satisfaction—but as part of a larger scheme to create a flashpoint culture in which employee motivation, too, is raised in parallel. Chapter 3 outlined a four-step process for beginning the shift toward a flashpoint culture:

1. Have employees come up with their own ideas to improve the customer experience.
2. Help the employees successfully implement their ideas.
3. Make it easy and convenient for customers to supply positive feedback about these ideas.
4. Use this feedback as the basis for employee recognition.

In a sense my 2006 Entrepreneur Press book *Customer Service Made Easy* can be thought of as a companion volume for this one. The other book provides detailed instructions for accomplishing Step One of the above process, as an employee-level strategy for gaining competitive advantage. By comparison, the emphasis in these pages is on accomplishing steps two, three, and four, but as a leadership-level strategy for *creating and reinforcing organizational alignment*. To put it another way, in the other book the object is to help managers and process facilitators most effectively engage their work teams in energizing the "customer satisfaction" side of the coin; here it's to help senior management most effectively energize the "employee motivation" side. Micro there, macro here. The flashpoint effect is what happens when both sides become so energized, the energy flows with a life of its own in a continuous circular motion from each to the other. (Though a certain amount of overlap in the two books is essential to ensure both readership groups have some understanding of what the other is doing— and how it all fits together to create the chain reaction effect—I've kept the duplication of content to an absolute minimum.)

The Big Disconnect

Many surveys have been developed over the years to help businesses measure current levels of employee motivation or morale. Sometimes they're referred to as attitude surveys, or employee satisfaction surveys. As an employee, you may have been asked to fill in one or more surveys of this type in the past. You may even have administered one or two for workers of your own over the years.

While most satisfaction surveys ask respondents to reveal their degree of satisfaction on the job, surprisingly few invite respondents to pinpoint what it is that *gives* them satisfaction on the job. Most surveys ask whether the employees feel motivated, but seldom ask what it is that actually motivates them. The survey designers and administrators presumably feel very confident they already know the answers to those questions. With most businesses driven by self-interest, it would follow that money would automatically be expected as the near-universal response. Yet consulting companies like Novations Group, which has done extensive survey work in hundreds of organizations for over 20 years, typically find otherwise. "Money is definitely not the biggest motivator of all," Novations' Peter Ambrozaitis* declares flatly. "Money is typically number six or seven on every survey I've ever seen done of actual associates throughout the years."[1]

Those rare surveys that *do* invite respondents to identify their biggest motivators usually do so through a multiple-choice question. Response

---

* Peter Ambrozaitis is regional vice president of sales at Boston-Based Novations Group Inc. Novations is a 30-plus-year-old training and consulting firm that works with most of the Fortune 100 companies throughout the United States. (Novations' wide range of products includes the *Customer Service From The Inside Out* program, co-developed with the author.) Peter joined Novations in 1999 as director of client services.

options typically include "higher wages" (of course), along with "management appreciation," "improvements in working conditions," "perks and incentives," "opportunities for advancement," and so on. When the designers of employee surveys prepare the multiple-choice list of candidates for biggest motivator, does it ever occur to them that they may have neglected to include one of the biggest of all on their list? Perhaps they added to the various response options an item such as "Other (please specify)," which may have given them some sense of reassurance that they'd allowed for all possibilities. But if every choice on the list of possible responses describes an *internal* motivator—something that originates from within the organization—is there not a danger that respondents will assume this question is deliberately limiting itself to internal motivators? Is it not likely that respondents who choose the "Other" option will be inclined (even if unconsciously) to list one or more internal motivators there too?

Reason I'm asking: any time I speak to workers in highly-motivated business settings, and ask them what *their* big motivator is, I always get the same reply. I don't box them in with a multiple-choice question, I don't preface the question by listing a bunch of internal motivators as examples of "right" answers. I just point-blank ask them what gives them the most satisfaction in their jobs, what fuels their determination to give their all day in and day out. For example, when I asked this of Camille Maxwell, office coordinator at the reservation call center at Delaware North's Parks & Resorts division, her answer was immediate: "Being able to get that [guest] into their accommodations that they've been trying *so hard* to get," she said. "I just like to call them and say, 'Hey, guess what—we got the room,' to [hear the guest] say, just, 'Thank you, Miracle Worker, you did it again!'"[2] It doesn't matter if I'm speaking to workers in the busiest Dunkin' Donuts in the world, or in a hotel, or in a telephone company, or in a retail store, or in a manufacturing plant, or anywhere—their answer is always the same. These energized businesses are invariably driven by an external focus on customers, and the biggie at the top of their hit parade is therefore an *external* motivator: positive customer feedback. The more direct and spontaneous the positive customer feedback is, the greater its motivational effect.

So why, then, does this option so seldom appear on employee surveys? Well that, of course, would be because hardly any businesses see a link between customer satisfaction and employee satisfaction. It's the big disconnect. Only those electrified, turbo-charged, *powerhouse* businesses have made the connection—and we all know how rare those businesses are. (The big disconnect is *why* they're so rare.) If there are any employee motivators to be found at all inside an organization with a predominantly internal focus on self-interest, these too will by necessity be mostly of the internal variety. Probably the simpler reason most surveys never mention positive customer feedback is because most businesses don't generate a whole lot of it to begin with, so neither the designers of the surveys nor their respondents are inclined to even think of it. And of course, the continuing absence of this key external motivator on such surveys helps perpetuate its absence in people's *mental* lists of major employee motivators as well.

The big disconnect is a slow, silent, invisible killer of businesses. It operates like an odorless poison gas, confounding the mind and clouding judgment. When its damage becomes apparent, the victims concoct their own explanations for it and implement their own remedies, which usually also do nothing to address root causes.

To cite a common example, consider the delegation problem. When the topic of delegation comes up in management courses, great pains are typically taken to impress upon students that it's ineffective to delegate tasks without also delegating the *responsibility* and *authority* for these tasks. Why after so many years does this remain such a difficult principle to ingrain in managers young and old? It's because this is really not a "delegation" issue at all. Delegation is small potatoes—this is a much deeper and more basic cultural issue around EIO, employee involvement and ownership. Most organizations see no direct link between customer satisfaction and employee motivation, most business schools never touch upon any such link, most business books and articles make no mention of it, so right across the entire business landscape there's just no compelling reason to develop a culture of EIO. The accepted view for most managers is that it's up to the training department to do something about raising customer service levels, and it's the HR department's responsibility to come up with incentive programs to keep workers motivated. And because this disjointed approach isn't working so well, these increasingly insecure managers come to feel they'd better cover their hindquarters by *personally* making sure things get done right—so they delegate tasks, but retain the responsibility for those tasks. Management insecurity is an epidemic in most of our organizations, precisely because the combination of low customer satisfaction and low employee motivation is crippling the bottom line and has everyone nervous and on edge. This is a classic downward spiral directly attributable to the big disconnect, invisible killer of businesses.

Step One of our four-step culture-shift process seems simple and straightforward enough, but my entire previous book revolves around how to implement it effectively. Carried to its logical conclusion, this step represents turning over full involvement and ownership for the customer experience to frontline employees. In organizational cultures poisoned by the big disconnect, this can be an almost terrifying prospect. Much of the previous book is devoted to reducing anxiety especially in those managers, supervisors, team leaders, and trainers who'll be facilitating the employee brainstorming sessions, and who (even if only unconsciously) may be uneasy about empowering their own employees to such an extent. This is also why in Chapter 3 of this book I introduced the four-step process as a four-step *experiment*. Let's not paralyze insecure managers with more fear—let's take it slow and easy, try out the four steps on a trial basis in one corner of the organization, and (as outlined in the previous chapter) let the change "sneak up" on people one benefit at a time. Does this mean it's going to take forever to create that turbo-charged workforce promised on the cover of this book? Not at all. In fact, as will be meaningful to anyone who understands the fable of the tortoise and the hare: THE QUICKEST WAY TO ACHIEVE CULTURAL CHANGE IS SLOWLY.

Evolution, not revolution. The histories of businesses are full of epic sagas in which leaders suddenly "get religion" about the need for some kind of profound culture change. Then they invest endless resources in a mammoth high-urgency implementation that meets with immediate resistance on all sides and ultimately collapses under its own weight before it can even get off the ground. Instantaneous culture change ends up taking forever to achieve, because it never "takes" at all.

The four-step process is the antidote to the big disconnect. It allows individual employees and managers to *experience* the connection between customer satisfaction and employee motivation for themselves. They begin experiencing it in the very first step, as part of brainstorming ideas to delight customers.

First Step: The Three Customer Focus Principles
Have employees come up with their own ideas to improve the customer experience.

The employee brainstorming sessions described in *Customer Service Made Easy* are designed to generate ideas for delighting customers in three ways. A facilitator leads participating employees through three consecutive rounds of creative question-and-answer interaction, and encourages the employees to write their ideas on Post-it® notes, which are transferred to the wall in a matrix—a structured arrangement of rows and columns to simplify later review and retrieval of ideas. This particular Customer Focus Process (CFP) has 20 years of application history behind it, in hundreds of organizations around the world; it's also the basis for the Novations *Customer Service From The Inside Out* program.

The three rounds of employee brainstorming each reflect one of three customer focus principles. These principles can be thought of as the behavioral characteristics of customer-focused businesses. That is to say, these are three things such businesses are *aligned* toward accomplishing on a routine day-to-day basis, while other businesses virtually never make even an effort to accomplish them.

1. Exceed the Customer's Expectations Every Step of the Way

The idea of exceeding expectations is what springs to mind for most people when they think of "superior service" or "delighting customers." But the objective in the opening round of CFP brainstorming is not just to come up with ideas for exceeding expectations in a *general way* (such as "be friendlier," or "be more helpful"). Instead, participants break a typical customer transaction into its individual chronological or procedural steps and uncover ways to exceed expectations *within each step* of the transaction. Getting down to this level of specificity tends to generate ideas that would never otherwise come to light. As an example, in the Irish Superquinn chain of supermarkets, customers leaving the store are provided with umbrellas to get them to their parked cars in wet weather.

2. Make the Customer Feel Important

As illustrated in the photos at the start of this chapter, many businesses openly express contempt for their customers. Every day in businesses of every kind, customers are made to feel like unwelcome intruders, annoying interruptions of the organization's "real" work, potentially dishonest invaders against whom the organization must take special precautions to protect itself. CFP's second round of brainstorming looks for ways to make customers feel valued and important in every step of the transaction. Participants also uncover things that should be discontinued or removed, in order to avoid directly or indirectly sending negative messages to customers. An example is the decision within Stage Stores (described in Chapter 4) to eliminate a check-validation procedure that may have been sending an unintended message of mistrust to customers.

3. Tailor the Experience to Fit the Customer

Most businesses routinely interact with customers of varying age groups, educational backgrounds, income levels, occupations, nationalities, and so on. Each of these customer categories—along with others specific to your industry or situation—may have expectations unique to itself. The third and final round of CFP brainstorming seeks to identify what these unique expectations might be, and what might be done to meet—or, where possible, exceed—them. An example might be a doctor's waiting room stocked with up-to-date magazines in various languages, to accommodate patients of differing nationalities. Ideas uncovered in this round are often of the kind that generate the most motivational forms of positive customer feedback.

While no actual training or "teaching" takes place in these employee brainstorming sessions, this does not mean no *learning* takes place. Participants often discover that many of their ideas represent simple, virtually effortless things to do—such as smile more, or address customers by name, or apologize for delays or errors. As the ideas accumulate during the session, participants also typically come to realize, entirely on their own, that many of these ideas have the real potential to transform the customer experience—and as a direct result, their own experience on the job as well. They begin to *anticipate* positive feedback from their customers, and its effect on themselves. Furthermore, regardless of how many useful ideas happen to emerge in any given brainstorming session, the structure of the interaction encourages participants to analyze all aspects of the customer experience from the customers' viewpoint. This exercise alone can be a revelation to many employees. Process facilitators often report observing their workers becoming more customer-focused right before their eyes, even before a single idea has been implemented.

It bears emphasizing, however, that the real power of this process derives from the fact that the emerging ideas are the employees' own, written in their own words, in their own handwriting. The ownership element changes everything. As Paula Davis, General Motors' Certified Administrator of Suggestion Systems (and a past president of the Employee Involvement Association) puts it, "It makes [workers] feel a part of where the company's going. It means that their job means something to them. They're contributing to the business through their engagement or their involvement in the company."3

"When we engage associates in coming up with their own ideas around improving customer service within their organization," says Novations' VP Peter Ambrozaitis, "there's a much higher level of motivation, because the ideas are coming from them, and they're able to hear from their customers how customer service has been improved at a particular restaurant, retail outlet, or hospitality location." Where does Peter's certainty come from? "Through post-brainstorming interviews, talking with the associates, and just hearing the enthusiasm that they have around the fact that their ideas are what has positively impacted the customer service experience."4

The reason employee ownership is so critical in this first step is to ensure that workers will also feel ownership for any positive customer feedback that ensues—which is the happy by-product when such feedback is in effect celebrating the workers' own creativity and personality. This is what makes these workers feel "useful and necessary in the world." This is what makes work deeply satisfying at the personal level.

This is therefore where Step Two comes into play.

Second Step: Implementation Support
Help the employees successfully implement their ideas.

A typical CFP employee brainstorming session will generate dozens of potentially useful ideas. The mere fact than an idea has been articulated and posted in the wall matrix, however, does not necessarily mean it will ultimately be implemented. Process facilitators know there aren't enough hours in the day to do all of these things. At the conclusion of the three rounds of brainstorming, the facilitator therefore invites participants to review their inventory of new ideas, and if they should feel so inclined, to each select one or more for implementation on a purely voluntary basis.

Managers who have not attended CFP brainstorming sessions, and whose broader experience with employee ownership may be limited, typically worry that keeping implementation on a voluntary basis means few if any ideas will be ultimately taken on as personal initiatives. From years of habit, such managers cannot resist the temptation to make the implementation of at least one-idea-per-participant mandatory. My own experience in countless such sessions, however, is that the ownership aspect works so well on a voluntary basis, the danger tends to be the opposite—some participants will tend to take on more initiatives than they can handle. Whereas, when implementation becomes mandatory, the whole process is made to feel like one more management effort to legislate behavior change. This undermines the ownership element completely, turning it from an employee-owned program right back into a management-owned program. Yes, there'll always be some workers in any given session who choose to take on no initiative at all. In an evolution-not-revolution approach to culture change, my recommendation is to let it pass. They'll come around once they see the effect of positive customer feedback on their peers. There'll be additional brainstorming sessions in the future; every employee will have a chance to become a hero in customers' eyes.

Not every idea selected for implementation will necessarily be cost-free, of course. In Chapter 3 I gave the example of worker Terry coming up with an idea to provide a bench for senior citizens. There will be some costs associated with acquiring and installing such a bench. Imagine another employee wanting to implement a program for giving customers free product samples. More cost. Another would like to improve the lighting in the customer waiting room and make a range of current magazines available. Still more cost. Step Two in our four-step process for culture change involves helping employees successfully implement their ideas—but what if there are more good ideas than the organization can afford to implement at any one time? And what if a given employee thinks his or her idea is fantastic, but we at a management level are aware of other factors that make it impractical or impossible? How do we handle killing employee initiatives where unavoidable, without killing employee motivation in the process?

The answers to these questions lie in establishing two elements that both relate to Step Two in our four-step process: the Flashpoint Fund, and the Grants Program.

Funding Motivation

It's an obvious and inevitable question: where's the money to fund all these wonderful ideas supposed to come from?

The first piece of good news is that you're probably already allocating the money to other things—things that at present may be working *against* organizational alignment. And the second even better piece of good news is that you need relatively little investment to get the culture change started. Once the four-step process comes to life, it quickly begins paying its own way, with generous dividends to boot.

Let's take a closer look at that first piece of good news. Do a little simple arithmetic in your head: about how much, roughly, does your business currently spend in an average year on various employee incentives, bonuses, prizes, perks, parties, or any other investments to boost morale and motivation? Now whatever that round figure may be, add to it the following: about how much do you spend per year on customer service training, or any other form of employee training designed to improve some or all aspects of the customer experience? Now kindly add one more figure: in ballpark terms, what is your typical annual budget for advertising, promotion, marketing, or any other investment to attract new customers to your business? Whatever your round-number total is when you tally these three figures together—there, right off the bat, is a figure some portion of which can be reallocated to the beginning of your culture change. The four-step process does a far better job of improving the customer experience than any customer service training. It also promotes employee motivation for more effectively than any incentive program. (Monies currently being poured into either of these as separate activities may actually be reinforcing the big disconnect.) The four-step process also generates positive word of mouth, that most effective—and least expensive—form of advertising on the planet.

So the *initial* cost of getting the flashpoint chain reaction started may already be budgeted for in other activities that the new culture will quickly render obsolete. And as we know, flashpoint businesses are invariably the most profitable—which clarifies where the funds to *sustain* the chain reaction will come from over the longer term.

But no matter how large or small the initial flashpoint fund may be, it remains possible (and even fairly likely) that employees will want to implement more service innovations than the fund can cover. That's where the grants program comes in.

Making the Case for Delight

The Customer Focus Process does not lead participating employees to assume that any idea they select for implementation at the end of brainstorming sessions will automatically be funded by their organization, regardless of cost, on a no-questions-asked basis. Instead, participants learn that it will be their responsibility to apply to management for a "funding grant" for any idea that entails direct or indirect costs.

The grants program involves applicants making as persuasive a case as they can for their particular idea: what exactly does it entail, how or why do they believe it will add delight to the customer experience, what is their estimate of total cost, how will they solicit and report customer feedback to confirm that the idea is having the desired effect, and so on.

These applications for funding can be made in a variety of ways, depending on the individual business culture. At the reserved-and-low-key end of the cultural spectrum, employees quietly submit their applications, in person or in writing, to the management team on an as-needed basis. In the more boisterous-and-fun kinds of cultures, the business holds special monthly or quarterly review meetings, with all employees in attendance, in which applicants present their case in as flamboyantly creative and entertaining a manner as they wish, using audio-visual support materials, and even theatrical skits that demonstrate their idea in use. (In this latter approach, the degree of laughter or applause from employees in the audience may influence management's decision to fund the implementation or not.)

The benefits that derive from establishing a grants program are considerable.

- The need to apply for funding reminds everyone that not every proposed idea can and will necessarily be implemented.
- It reduces the impression that the awarding of funding is entirely arbitrary, on the basis of management whim.
- The need for applicants to estimate implementation costs gives them a strong incentive to uncover ways to *reduce* costs, in order to better their chances of securing funding.
- Because applicants must propose their own implementation procedures, their sense of personal involvement and ownership is further enhanced.
- Besides indicating to management less-obvious ways in which proposed ideas may "wow" customers, the applicants' presentations also hint, through the degree of energy and conviction poured into them, which ideas are most potentially motivational for the employees themselves—a key consideration.
- To make the case for their idea, its champions must put themselves squarely in the customers' shoes—a powerful exercise in "customer-focused thinking" in its own right.
- (In the more flamboyant cultures) the entire application process itself becomes another "fun" workplace activity associated with the shift

toward a more customer-focused culture. It promotes healthy competitive rivalries among employees, who in subsequent brainstorming and grant-application events will strive to outshine their peers with ideas that are more inventive, and presentations that are more memorable and entertaining.

- The need for applicants to define in advance how customer feedback will be collected and reported sets the stage for the greatest motivational payoff possible.

Based on the quantity and quality of applications, and the amount of funding available, management awards grants to those ideas that seem most likely to generate positive customer feedback, or otherwise give the implementers the greatest motivational boost. Those whose ideas did not receive a grant this time around are encouraged to try again next time.

As part of awarding the funding for a particular idea or project, management in advance stipulates a schedule for regular "progress reports" from the implementers. The purpose of these is to avoid being seen as standing over the workers' shoulders, while at the same time making it easier to virtually *ensure* that the implementation will be a howling success. It means being especially alert for signs that unexpected complications or problems have cropped up, and then offering to help find solutions if and when they do. For example, if the implementers discover some kind of signage is needed, and the business has a graphics technician or department, management formally makes that resource available to them. The implementers need permission to work late on the project one evening—management grants it, and perhaps even arranges pizza delivery for the nighthawks. Generating raves from delighted customers is the ultimate goal here, and management does all it can to ensure that successful implementation of the initiative will unleash raves galore.

Third Step: Harvesting Feedback
Make it easy and convenient for customers to supply positive feedback about these ideas.

Not all delighted customers will automatically express their pleasure in the form of direct feedback. Many will be content to show their appreciation simply by returning to conduct repeat business. Nor will all employees who deliver delight automatically seek out positive feedback on their own initiative. Many will be content to interpret the high volume of repeat business to mean customers are sufficiently satisfied.

Managers in flashpoint cultures, however, are typically *not* content to let things ride in this unspoken way. They recognize that motivational opportunities are being missed. To fully appreciate what these managers do, it helps to understand the hidden function of applause.

Anthropologist Desmond Morris may have been the first to suggest that applause represents collective back-patting from a distance. The sound of clapping hands might be a way by which each member of an appreciative audience can convey, "This is what I would be doing on your back if I could be near you right now." Professional stage performers know all about the power of applause. Orators pause in their speeches to encourage applause, actors and musicians take a bow at the ends of various sections of their performances to do the same. Circus acrobats follow every routine with a flourish—one or both hands raised beside and slightly above the head in a graceful ballet-like gesture, a "cue to applaud." The cue for audiences in TV studios is an actual APPLAUSE sign that flashes at the touch of a button, to leave nothing to chance.

What if a stage artist delivered an amazing performance, but at its conclusion *discouraged* applause from the audience? When classical music is being recorded in a live concert hall setting, the conductor or producer will sometimes ask the audience not to applaud at the end, at least until the very last notes have died away and an "all clear" signal is given. Audiences find it hard *not* to applaud after a superb performance. If there were to be no applause at all—if the audience was expected simply to get up and quietly head home—there'd be a sense of letdown. The cheering and the hoopla are part of what makes the concert experience satisfying for performer and audience alike. Remove this element, and the audience can feel disappointed.

Unlike show-biz folk, the rest of us can sometimes feel somewhat awkward and self-conscious when we're the object of applause. We tend to automatically put up our hands in a silencing gesture, as if pleading with the applauders to stop at once.

Our intention may be to exhibit modesty and humility—but in depriving others of their opportunity to applaud us, we may unknowingly be cheating them of something they've been looking forward to. We may be unknowingly lessening their sense of enjoyment about expressing their appreciation, and even the extent to which they'll look back on the moment as a fully satisfying one for them. Strange as it may seem, it can sometimes be an act of generosity to give others an opportunity to express their gratitude to us. It's what those in show-biz have known all along, and the rest of us must learn: often the hidden function of applause is to make the *applauder* feel good.

Managers in flashpoint businesses may not be doing it consciously, but when they create comfortable (that is, nonawkward) opportunities for delighted customers to spontaneously *express* that delight, they're often actually further enhancing the customer experience.

Applicants seeking funding for an idea or project that derives from CFP brainstorming are required, as a nonnegotiable part of the process, to define *how they themselves intend to go about collecting customer feedback about their idea*, and how they will subsequently report highlights of this feedback to management. This policy serves two important purposes. First, as a further form of employee ownership, it makes the implementers responsible for validating the basic effectiveness of the idea or project, while also providing a safeguard against any unanticipated negative side effects for customers. Second, it ensures that implementers will derive the maximum motivational benefit of spontaneous feedback from delighted customers.

How are employees to go about collecting such feedback? In cultures that are more subdued, implementers might for example hand customers a special "feedback card" that limits itself to specific questions about the new idea or project. The customers fill these out at their leisure; management later receives an oral or written summary of the feedback cards' content. In boisterous high-energy cultures, implementers might use a camcorder to make documentary-style recordings of customers expressing their sponta-neous delight and screen this footage for management and employees in a subsequent grant-application review meeting. By reminding grant appli-cants that the effectiveness of their proposed feedback collection-and-reporting strategy may influence the decision to award funding, management can encourage employees to adopt a more creative and "fun" approach with this aspect of the process as well.

Case Study in Feedback Collection

One of the most thorough—and effectively used—mechanisms for collect-ing spontaneous customer feedback this writer has encountered is the elec-tronic customer survey built into Delaware North's *GuestPath* program.

According to Stewart Collins, on a monthly basis about 25 thousand parties currently check out of the Parks & Resorts division's 11 properties. These parties naturally provide their e-mail addresses when making reser-vations, to receive e-mail confirmation. "We send out an electronic invita-tion to every guest that stays with us," Stewart explains, "an invitation to participate in a survey. And we ask every single one. This isn't a 'sample'—everybody is invited to participate." The invitation thanks the guest for vis-iting and provides a one-click link to the survey. About 38 percent of guests currently complete the survey, says Stewart. "So as you can imagine, I've got data—*beaucoup* amounts of data."

How elaborate is the survey? "It's not short," he says. "It takes 15 to 20 minutes to complete. It easily has a hundred questions." This is making it easy and convenient for customers to supply feedback? "I think we get good response," he says, "because this is part of [their] guest experience, and by them completing the survey it contributes to their experience." (To put it another way, it gives the audience a welcome opportunity to applaud [or boo] while their feelings about the experience remain at their strongest.) As a further incentive, "There's a six-thousand-dollar sweepstakes they're entered into. And we do the six thousand quarterly, so it's 25 thousand over the course of the year. But the chances of winning are not sky-high, [because] so many people participate."

How do the proportions of favorable and unfavorable feedback break out? "For every hundred complaints," he says, "I get about 75 compliments of staff." It means at this point in the evolution of the company's *GuestPath* program, negative comments outnumber positive ones. But as Stewart is quick to point out, not so long ago, when standard "comment cards" were the primary feedback mechanism, virtually *all* the feedback was negative—which of course is the kind of stimulus that inspires a company to create a program like *GuestPath* in the first place.

"The survey is comprised of essentially four components," Stewart explains. "There's a *loyalty* component: how likely are you to buy from us again, how likely are you to recommend us to a friend—which is probably the most important question—and then what was your satisfaction. Then there's a big section in the middle about measuring to the *GuestPath* standards. A very powerful majority of the questions are there. Then there's a section of, 'Hey, is there an associate who you'd like pick out that really did something really well?'" Stewart repeats the last phrase for emphasis: "*Really well*—we don't ask did they do something bad. Somebody that you'd like to point out that was exceptional. So we get a huge return on recognition of associates. *Huge.* I'm tickled pink that it happens, but I'm kind of blown away that it's that big. And then the last part [of the survey] is that kind of 'service recovery' problem: what happened, how could we be better, whatever."

Stewart then explains how the incoming feedback is handled, using his name and mine to illustrate. "If Stewart did a great job," he says, "and Paul filled out this e-survey and wrote me down by name, this piece [pointing to one section of the survey on his computer screen] gets printed, and handed to the associate, and thanked, and this is ... " He pauses. "I don't want to say it's instantaneous, but it is very fast. Paul checked out on Sunday, we invite him to fill out the survey on Monday, he completes the survey on Tuesday, and on Tuesday afternoon you get a recognition from a guest that checked out last week. Incredibly powerful." What kind of effect does it have? "Those properties that are doing that consistently," he says, "their morale has just taken off. Phenomenal. Because they touched the guest. There's a connection—so much so that the guest recognized them by name. We have properties where there's competitions—informal, not by management, by the associates: 'I'm going to get more than you this month.' Incredibly powerful. And immediate. Immediate feedback is the key here."

As Stewart points out, the usefulness of this tool does not end with recognition. "The next section [of the survey] is that problem resolution component. Obviously, [as a] soft business, we have problems with associates. You're also able to take that [printout] and go sit with that associate, and coach them, ultimately maybe discipline them, or guide them down the right path—but we can close those gaps." He once again uses his own name to illustrate: "So, Stewart didn't give a great guest experience, it's not Stewart's boss coming and saying, 'Hey, what the heck happened here?' It's, 'This came in from our guest last night. It's Mr. Turner that checked out of the room, and you cleaned his room, and he's not happy with the way his room was cleaned.' The associate can't really argue at that point. Certainly they [may] get defensive, or whatever, but there's none of that emotional component that takes place between a manager and the associate. This is the opinion that the guest had. Right, wrong, or indifferent, this is their opinion. In our business, their opinion is more 'right' than right is."

Stewart turns to his computer and opens a file on his screen to demonstrate a design feature of the survey software. "There are triggers in the surveys," he says, "that send out alerts programmed to the appropriate manager to recognize their associate, or that there was a problem that took place. So those alerts come through the e-mail system." He indicates a small number on his screen. "Right now I have 20, from the last—" He pauses to glance at the clock on the wall. "How long have we been sitting here? An hour? Okay, [in that hour] 20 have come in from 11 different properties across the country. So I can open one of these up—let's just open this one from Wawona." As I watch, he opens an e-mail alert that has arrived from the Wawona Hotel, one of the company's properties at California's Yosemite National Park, and begins reading directly from the screen. "Okay, so this guest says, *'I would like to commend your restaurant staff on excellent and friendly service. Your staff made me feel comfortable and at ease with their intelligent and comfortable manner of engaging conversation or leaving the guest in peace. In particular, Mathew Key was an excellent server; competent and friendly, attentive and flexible. Thanks for a great experience.'* Now I tell you what," Stewart says, "you print that out, and you go and hand it to Mathew *right now*. It came in at—" He once more consults his computer screen. "8:44, what time is it now? 9:40. Within an hour I go hand it to Mathew. Mathew's *struttin'*. No question. He's puffed up. How could he not be?"

Back to the computer screen. "I'll see if I can find a negative one," he says, scrolling. "Okay, so here's a negative one. Marilyn [K.] completed this at 7:49 this morning. She wrote that the room wasn't available upon request. She still had a pretty good time, [a score of] 'fours' across the board on a scale of one-to-five, so a pretty good experience, but she was kind enough to tell us that the room wasn't available upon her arrival. The general manager at Tenaya [the Tenaya Lodge at Yosemite] could call ..." (He reads off the digits of the customer's telephone number.) "... right now— because chances are she's still close to home—pick it up and say, 'Mrs. [K.], I am so sorry that your room wasn't ready when you checked in. We dropped the ball. And that affected your experience. It's important to me that I know that—I thank you for bringing it to my attention. The next time you come back we are going to exceed your expectations.'"

Would a response as speedy as this be typical? "The manager has to respond to all complaints within 48 hours," Stewart says. "As an aside, we're not quite there yet, but the standard is 48 hours. Let's say that she had said that the experience wasn't that great. I could go back and open up her survey and see how she responded to every single question, and I could call her back and say, 'You know, I notice that you really didn't have a great experience, you said your room wasn't ready, but you also said the dining room experience wasn't very good.' Now how powerful is that—you call a guest within a couple of hours of them completing a survey. Let's say Mathew did a bad job, you could go back to Mathew and hand him the same thing and say, 'You know, a guest felt that you ignored them. What are we going to do to close that gap?' And really work to close that gap."

He consults his computer screen one more time. "In this last month," he says, "we had about 25 hundred responses to the surveys. I can go through and tell you how many customer comments we had. It's staggering."[5]

Stewart Collins works with this tool every day, and he's *still* bowled over by the power of the customer feedback it collects to reinforce alignment within his company.

Fourth Step: The Motivational Payoff
Use this feedback as the basis for employee recognition.

This is the payoff portion of the four-step process for culture change. While positive customer feedback fresh and hot off the presses is the big motivator, flashpoint businesses don't limit their employees to a one-time dosage. They create "time-release motivators," as we'll explore in more detail in Chapter 7.

The intent is to put this feedback to work not only as a motivator of employees, but also as a force for cultural alignment. For example, if the general employee population does not attend funding-application review meetings—an ideal forum for celebrating successes, as we'll explore more fully in Chapter 7—then management creates other opportunities for the entire workforce to cheer and applaud customer reaction to the implementers' new idea or project. If the feedback is in written form, a prominent bulletin board is established to showcase it to employees (and to visitors from outside the organization as well). If the business is involved in advertising and promotional activities, some of the customer feedback finds it way into these materials. (Where the feedback cites one or more employees by name, this kind of promotional material makes those employees mini-celebrities in the community at large.) A journalistic-type "story" on the project, its implementer(s), and the reactions of customers appears in the company newsletter, the annual report, or any other appropriate form of internal communication. In some cases, the organization may incorporate the implementer's name into all references to the idea or project: "We'll be installing more of Terry's benches-for-seniors in several of our other locations this summer."

Through it all, management stands in the shadows and makes its own contribution to the success virtually invisible. The spotlight is entirely on the implementers alone. They're made to look and feel like heroes in the eyes of customers—and in the eyes of their peers as well.

Once the four-step process is set in motion, with workers coming up with their own new ways to deliver delight, and happy customers supplying positive feedback to encourage the workers to continue, management can step back and consider a few key elements to help the whole process run smoothly.

One such element is the establishment of a reliable measurement system to track progress, as we'll see next.

Notes

1. Peter Ambrozaitis, Novations Group, interview with the author, December 28, 2006.
2. Camille Maxwell, DNC, interview with the author, October 31, 2006.
3. Paula Davis, General Motors, interview with the author, December 4, 2006.
4. Peter Abrozaitis interview.
5. Stewart Collins, DNC, interview with the author, October 31, 2006.

Chapter 6

Measuring Progress Toward Alignment

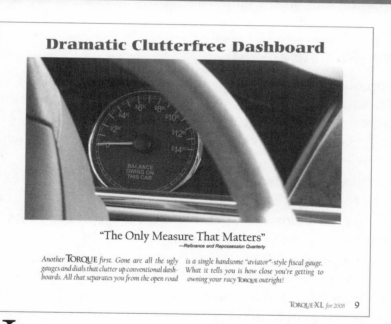

Dramatic Clutterfree Dashboard

BALANCE OWING ON THIS CAR

"The Only Measure That Matters"
—Refinance and Repossession Quarterly

Another TORQUE first. Gone are all the ugly gauges and dials that clutter up conventional dashboards. All that separates you from the open road is a single handsome "aviator"-style fiscal gauge. What it tells you is how close you're getting to owning your racy TORQUE outright!

TORQUE-XL for 2008   9

"**W**e are phenomenal at measuring financial results," says DNC's Stewart Collins. "I mean, we are phenomenal at it. In fact we might be so good at it that it gets in the way of some of the other things that are really more important."[1] More important than financial results? Is there really anything that could possibly be more important than that?

We call them financial "results," of course, because they're the result of something prior. They're what you're left with, after the fact. They provide an excellent rear-view-mirror indicator of where you've been.

Businesses aspiring to develop a flashpoint culture need to track where they're *going* more than where they've been. They use such measures to *ensure* a happy financial result. They must track employee motivation, since in a flashpoint culture this is what drives up customer satisfaction. And they must also track customer satisfaction, since in such a culture this is what drives up employee motivation. By confirming through measurement that both halves of the flashpoint equation are improving in tandem, they monitor their progress toward organizational alignment. The first half of this chapter focuses on the employee motivation half of the equation.

Data vs. Measurement

The big problem with standard employee surveys, according to Novations' Cathi Rittelmann,* is that "... we're asking [employees] how satisfied they are. Satisfaction is just end result—it's not what you feel when you're engaged. It has nothing to do with motivation. Satisfied is what you feel after Thanksgiving dinner."[2]

Furthermore, Cathi believes, most such surveys play it safe by avoiding potentially troubling realities. In her words, they're not "... asking any questions that have any risk at all to them. It's typically yes-no questions: 'how long have you been with the organization, do you like what you do, on a scale of 1 to 10 rate how satisfied you are with the training and development you get' ... all of that sort of flat-line stuff. Which has everything to do with how I feel today, and nothing to do about how I got to feeling this way. Anybody could develop one of those, and manipulate the data in any-which-way you want—I'm just not sure what it tells you. Because if it reinforces what you already wanted it to reinforce, which is, [for example], 'Seventy-three-point-two percent of the people are satisfied with their jobs,'

---

* Cathi Rittelmann is vice president of curriculum and design at Novations Group Inc. She served as an independent consultant for the first dozen or so of her 15 years with the company.

then you're probably going to fold your hands and say, 'Gawd, we're good.' Or, 'Since turnover's 35 percent, we're [okay], the ones who aren't satisfied are leaving.'"[3]

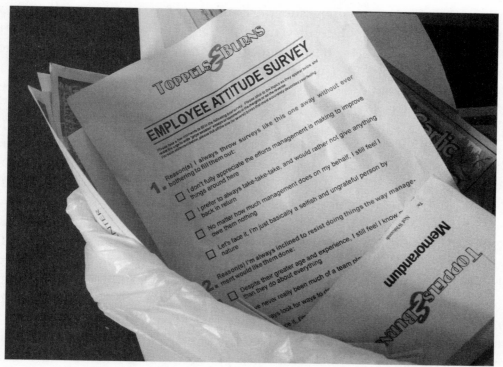

Measurement is a big topic—as a one-time trainer in Statistical Process Control at a Motorola plant outside Toronto, this I know very well. If current customer dissatisfaction in your organization is the product of internal systems and processes that are out of whack, you'll need measurement tools far more robust than those outlined below to make things right. The surveys discussed below provide a means to track progress—movement—in the organizational culture. They do not provide a means for measuring process efficiencies or product quality.

Measuring "progress" is not what most conventional surveys are designed to do at all. Their function is more typically to capture a single stand-alone "snapshot in time." Data is collected in order to provide some sense of what the organizational climate happens to be right then and there. The more detailed and complex the data in such a one-time snap-shot, the more it needs to be "interpreted"—and the greater the danger of differing interpretations, conflicting interpretations, inconclusive interpre-tations. In many companies, super-elaborate (and costly) internal surveys produce a mountain of results no one has time enough to fully sort through and digest. The results end up in the "survey cemetery"—some dusty storeroom where they await their eventual date with the shredder.

When you set out to measure anything at all, you inevitably end up with data. But this does not mean that when you set out to simply collect data, you always end up with a useful measure of anything. Let's use a vari-able such as "number of complaints per month" to illustrate. The statement *"We received 11 customer complaints last month"* is an example of raw data. What the data does not reveal is whether such a finding is noteworthy in some way. To answer that, we also need to know how many complaints are *typically* received per month. And even that does not allow us to determine whether the latest data indicates any kind of trend we should be aware of. For that, we'd need to know how many complaints were actually received the month before, and the month before that as well. The data becomes meaningful when we can say, "We received 11 customer complaints this month. This is less than half the number we received the month prior, and roughly a third of the number received the month before that. Last year our overall average was over 50 complaints per month." The actual individual monthly figures become eclipsed by a bigger story—the *trend* they reveal when considered together.

Our ultimate objective is to gradually bring our organization's culture into alignment. We need to be able to measure our progress over time. The only way to measure the progress of anything is to take a given measure-ment repeatedly, at regular intervals. Those monster once-every-blue-moon internal surveys try to accomplish too much. As a result usually they end up accomplishing very little. Instead of making a huge investment to estab-lish precisely how motivated our employees are feeling at a single point in time, down to the ninth decimal place, it's more useful to find out if over-all they're feeling *more* motivated now than they did three months ago—and if that in turn was better than how they felt three months earlier.

So to make our internal survey as useful as possible, we need to structure the actual questions in a way that will keep things simple. We'll want to redistribute the same survey several times a year, in order to track the trend toward alignment. As Mark Emmitte of Stage Stores puts it, "If you ask the right questions, in a way that people feel comfortable giving you honest answers, we feel that it is a very powerful way to determine [if] your culture [is] aligned with what you say."[4]

The Six Flashpoint Factors

In executive workshops like the one Mark's leadership team at Stage Stores went through, six "flashpoint factors" serve as the basis for six rounds of strategic planning for culture change.* The six factors together constitute a kind of planning checklist, a template to ensure that no key element is overlooked when businesses set out to take control of their organizational culture and transform it in some way. The book in your hands, too, loosely uses these same six flashpoint factors as the basis for its overall chapter-by-chapter structure. For measurement purposes, the flashpoint factors relate to six key parameters that need to be monitored as part of any effort to change an organizational culture. It's only as survey scores in all six areas begin to improve that the organization can be assured it's moving toward the flashpoint effect, the ultimate indicator of total alignment.

Note that the survey that comes out of this approach is not intended to be a scientifically rigorous measure of objective cultural realities. Instead, it's an informal measure of *perceptions*, which by definition are entirely subjective. For example, while it may not be easy to measure the extent to which employees are actually empowered and engaged within a given organization, it's relatively easy to measure the extent to which they *feel* empowered and engaged. Our purpose with these "culture surveys" would be to track the degree to which that feeling is increasing or decreasing over a given period of time.

---

* For the benefit of readers who may be interested, there are over 70 pages devoted to management-level planning exercises around these same flashpoint factors in the book *Customer Service Made Easy*.

From years of experience with "once-in-a-blue-moon" surveys, managers will often be inclined to place a great deal of importance on the actual scores such surveys each generate individually. Let's say the first time workers are asked about how empowered they feel, the aggregate score (on a scale from 1 to 10) is 2, and the second time, it's moved to 4. Managers may feel an urge to challenge these numbers, suggesting that a score of 2.3 in the first case and something closer to 4.7 or 4.8 in the second would be more "accurate." But it bears emphasizing—for our purposes, the accuracy of the individual scores is almost incidental. What matters is that by the time of the second survey, employees are by and large feeling *twice* as empowered as before. This is their perception and as such is not really open to debate. When we're tracking progress, it's the direction and degree of change that's important. And in this example, all managers should unequivocally see this degree of change as cause for celebration.

Assigning a simple numerical scale to the questions makes it easy to redistribute the same survey several times a year and compare the overall scores. Although sample questions are provided below within each of the six flashpoint factors, these questions are intended purely as examples, purely as a starting point. (You can imagine a 10-box scale similar to the following appended to each of the sample questions listed below.

I've omitted the actual scale after each sample question in these pages, to save space. Also, I acknowledge that my sample questions are not really questions at all—they're statements. They only *become* questions in combination with their accompanying numerical scale, which in effect is asking, "To what extent to you agree or disagree with this statement?" The actual wording of the questions in your version of the survey will almost certainly differ from those below, depending on various cultural aspects within your business. You may choose to use some of the samples "as is," or eliminate some of them, or add more, or even replace all of the samples with alternatives more suited to your unique situation. One note of caution, however—do not eliminate a question from your survey simply because it refers to an activity (such as employee brainstorming) that does not currently take place in your business. If you intend to *make it* part of your business at some point, the question should stay in the survey. Yes, your initial scores for such questions will probably hit rock-bottom, but the lower the scores at the beginning of the culture shift, the more gains you'll be able to celebrate as the scores improve. Similarly, resist the temptation to take out *any* question solely on the basis that it's likely to produce an "embarrassingly low" score at the outset. The first survey is your "before" picture. Once again, the more dramatic the improvement in the "after" picture, the more cause for celebration.

As you review the sample questions, you may have another concern about referring to activities the respondents have neither engaged in nor even heard about yet. From an internal communications standpoint, isn't this prematurely letting the cat out of the bag? To the contrary, such questions tucked into a survey are an excellent way to help these kinds of activities "sneak up" on the workforce without making any kind of big splashy announcement about them. And you may discover some workers are already doing things they consider quite similar to what the survey is alluding to. Thus you get better scores than you might have anticipated.

On a related matter, depending on the level of employee cynicism in your organization, you may get more reliable results from this kind of survey if you give respondents the option of retaining their anonymity.

One last note—to keep respondents alert, it's advisable to mix in some questions for which a *decreasing* score indicates a positive trend. The third sample question, below, is an example.

On to the six flashpoint factors.

1. Leadership

Flashpoint cultures never happen by happy accident. They must be *made* to happen. The leaders of an organization must make a conscious, deliberate decision to bring such a culture into being. The first three chapters of this book summarize the various aspects of such a decision. These include the decision to make work feel more like play for employees; the decision to replace a collective internal focus on self-interest with a more motivational external focus on customers' interests; and the decision to give employees a much greater sense of involvement and ownership for the customer experience.

The first sample questions in our measurement survey, therefore, are designed to track employee perceptions as they directly or indirectly relate to these three leadership elements.

1. I feel a sense of personal pride when talking about my company or my job with family and friends. 1 2 3 4 5 6 7 8 9 10

2. When I describe my job to family and friends, I often use words like "enjoyable" and "fun." 1 2 3 4 5 6 7 8 9 10

3. I believe the number one objective in this company is to make more money. 1 2 3 4 5 6 7 8 9 10

4. I believe the number one objective in this company is to help and please customers. 1 2 3 4 5 6 7 8 9 10

5. I always have a clear understanding of what my boss expects my number one priority on the job to be. 1 2 3 4 5 6 7 8 9 10

6. I routinely get immediate feedback on the job from my boss that lets me know how well I'm doing. 1 2 3 4 5 6 7 8 9 10

7. I routinely get immediate feedback on the job from customers that lets me know how well I'm doing. 1 2 3 4 5 6 7 8 9 10

8. The more positive the feedback is, the more satisfying my job becomes. 1 2 3 4 5 6 7 8 9 10

9. The company gives me opportunities to offer my own ideas on how to better help or please customers. 1 2 3 4 5 6 7 8 9 10

10. The company helps me implement my ideas for improving the customer experience. 1 2 3 4 5 6 7 8 9 10

11. The company lets me take full credit for my ideas and for my work in general. 1 2 3 4 5 6 7 8 9 10

12. Knowing I've helped customers in some way gives me a satisfying feeling of accomplishment. 1 2 3 4 5 6 7 8 9 10

2. Internal Communication

As outlined in Chapter 4, in flashpoint businesses the standard channels of internal communication exist not primarily for the dissemination of critical information, but more often to reinforce cultural alignment. It's therefore useful to have a mechanism for measuring progress toward this goal. (In the sample questions below, the word "newsletter" can be replaced by any other relevant internal communication tool[s].)

1. I would like management to do a better job of keeping the rest of us "in the know." 1 2 3 4 5 6 7 8 9 10

2. I feel a lot of the content in the employee newsletter does not really relate to me or my job. 1 2 3 4 5 6 7 8 9 10

3. The stories in our newsletter show how we're all working together to accomplish the same thing. 1 2 3 4 5 6 7 8 9 10

4. Reading the newsletter always makes me feel like I'm part of a winning team. 1 2 3 4 5 6 7 8 9 10

5. I can tell my coworkers enjoy being featured in newsletter success stories. 1 2 3 4 5 6 7 8 9 10

6. The stories in our newsletter prove our company is doing things that matter to our customers. 1 2 3 4 5 6 7 8 9 10

7. I feel a special sense of pride when my name or picture appears in the newsletter. 1 2 3 4 5 6 7 8 9 10

8. The stories in our newsletter prove that pleasing customers is the most important priority in this company. 1 2 3 4 5 6 7 8 9 10

3. Customer Delight

In Chapter 5 the emphasis is on delighting customers in order to harvest positive customer feedback as a powerful employee motivator. The object in the next section of our internal survey is to measure just *how* motivational the organization's emphasis on customer delight is proving to be for the employees involved. Not too many questions are required to paint that picture.

1. I feel proud to work for a company that always puts its customers first. 1 2 3 4 5 6 7 8 9 10

2. Management says customer satisfaction is the most important thing, but I sometimes see signs that some managers don't really feel that way. 1 2 3 4 5 6 7 8 9 10

3. I find group brainstorming sessions (to come up with ideas to improve things for customers) stimulating and rewarding.
1 2 3 4 5 6 7 8 9 10

4. I believe the companies that treat their customers best are always the ones that are most successful. 1 2 3 4 5 6 7 8 9 10

5. Management trusts me enough to let me handle customers in my own way. 1 2 3 4 5 6 7 8 9 10

6. This is a company that always tries to make its employees look good in customers' eyes. 1 2 3 4 5 6 7 8 9 10

7. The most satisfying part of my job is hearing from customers how much they appreciate the extra effort we (or I) make for them.
1 2 3 4 5 6 7 8 9 10

4. Measurement

A measurement for measurement? Yes, if we're going to invest time and resources in surveys as described in this chapter, we need to be able to confirm that they, too, are helping promote cultural alignment. To put it another way, this is a measure of the extent to which our efforts to track customer satisfaction and employee motivation are *contributing* to employee motivation.

1. I believe regular surveys like this one are a good way for companies to make sure their employees are feeling motivated.
1 2 3 4 5 6 7 8 9 10

2. I enjoy speaking directly to customers and asking for their impressions and reactions to what we do. 1 2 3 4 5 6 7 8 9 10

3. I believe we should create many opportunities for customers to share their feedback. 1 2 3 4 5 6 7 8 9 10

4. Filling out this survey makes me feel my company genuinely cares about my opinions and my perceptions. 1 2 3 4 5 6 7 8 9 10

5. Recognition

Virtually no one disputes the motivational effect of recognition in the workplace. As we'll see in the next chapter, however, some forms of recognition are more effective than others. The next few questions in our employee survey are designed to help us assess the motivational impact of our recognition efforts.

---

1. I sometimes feel no one appreciates the extra effort I put into my work.
   1 2 3 4 5 6 7 8 9 10

2. I get a pat on the back more often in this company than I ever did in any other place I ever worked. 1 2 3 4 5 6 7 8 9 10

3. Some managers in this company tend to be a little stingy with their praise. 1 2 3 4 5 6 7 8 9 10

4. I feel my contribution to this company is noted and valued.
   1 2 3 4 5 6 7 8 9 10

---

6. Operations

The last of the flashpoint factors, explored in Chapter 8, addresses the various operational systems, policies, processes, and procedures that collectively add up to "the way things are done around here." The object is to uncover any operational elements that may be working against cultural alignment, in order to be able to eliminate or revise these as necessary.

Management groups typically have a pretty good idea what's causing most employee and customer resistance in their organization. Because customer dissatisfaction inevitably contributes to employee dissatisfaction, in a survey designed to measure internal alignment, those cultural elements that frustrate both groups need to be specified. In some cases this could represent quite a list. The sample questions below give examples of how some of these might be included; not all of these may apply in your case. Conversely, there may be others that belong in your survey that do not appear below.

Cathi Rittelmann earlier made a reference to surveys that avoid "questions that have any risk at all to them." This part of the survey, in particular, is where what many managers will consider "risky" issues are brought into the open. There may be concern about opening a hornet's nest with questions that relate to systems or policies the company could not easily change even if it wanted to.

I will resist launching into a sermonette about "demonstrating leadership commitment," or managing change on a "leading by example" basis. The fundamental issue is employee motivation—turning an apathetic, cynical, disenfranchised workforce into an enthusiastic team driven by a shared objective. If we can point to sources of demotivation in our culture, elements over which the employees themselves have little or no control, and we find the prospect of tackling these too scary even to contemplate—well, then, perhaps a flashpoint culture is not destined to be part of our immediate future. On the brighter side, however, if we find *ourselves* resisting this kind of change, this should subsequently make it far easier for us to understand why our workers, too, tend to resist changes we would like them to embrace—even when these changes have the potential of making things better for everybody. So at least *that* one big mystery gets nicely cleared up.

1. Customers like our existing refunds and returns policy.
   1 2 3 4 5 6 7 8 9 10

2. When people are being hired for new positions, this company makes sure to hire only people who "fit in" well, and who really care about what the company stands for and is trying to accomplish.
   1 2 3 4 5 6 7 8 9 10

3. Customers find our business hours convenient. 1 2 3 4 5 6 7 8 9 10

4. I usually come away feeling a bit discouraged or frustrated from performance evaluation meetings with my boss. 1 2 3 4 5 6 7 8 9 10

5. Our customers find it difficult to contact the person in the company they want to talk to. 1 2 3 4 5 6 7 8 9 10

6. I like this company's sick-leave and time-off policies.
   1 2 3 4 5 6 7 8 9 10

7. Most managers in this company are good at keeping employees motivated and energized. 1 2 3 4 5 6 7 8 9 10

8. My company offers excellent opportunities for advancement and "promotes from within" wherever possible. 1 2 3 4 5 6 7 8 9 10

> **9. New employees are given an effective orientation that helps make them feel at home and among friends.** 1 2 3 4 5 6 7 8 9 10

A simple employee survey with questions relating to all six flashpoint factors, distributed at regular intervals, becomes an effective way to measure cultural progress toward alignment from the *employee* side of the fence.

Now over to the customer side.

The Three-Ring Model

As suggested above, the kinds of tools under discussion in this chapter do not measure objective absolutes. The measures described below will not record "number of wrong or incomplete shipments," for example, or "number of faulty or deficient products delivered," or "number of billing errors"—all of which will of course have a dramatic effect on customers' perception of our business. We could say these three examples represent "inner ring" issues. Our emphasis when measuring progress toward cultural alignment will be more on "outer ring" considerations.

If I may explain ...

About 20 years ago I began using a simple three-ring model (codeveloped in its original form with Art McNeil) to equip client organizations to untangle the ambiguities around phrases like "customer service" and "perception of value."

What's so ambiguous? Well, let's think about a business like a taxi service. If their basic product is a service, does "improving product quality" for them mean the same thing as "improving customer service"? Or how about the confusing notion of "internal customers?" Many organizations have an accounting department, for instance; when talk in this department turns to improving customer service, who are we describing as the customer? How do phrases like "return business" and "competitive advantage" apply to so-called internal customers? If they don't apply, does it mean employees who have no direct contact with external customers need not be concerned about helping to generate return business or competitive advantage for the organization as a whole? What does *that* do to organizational alignment?

The three-ring model replaces such ambiguities with simple straightforward language anyone at any level of an organization can understand and relate to. This is its power—to provide a common language that clearly distinguishes between "hard" and "soft" aspects of customer perception.* The model uses the word *customer* to refer to only one category of individual: someone outside the organization who is free to choose between availing him- or herself of the basic products or services we provide, or of seeking these (or an equivalent) elsewhere.

The model uses three concentric rings to visually represent how customers' perception of value can be made to contract or expand. When in these pages we refer to cultural alignment, we're describing a business culture in which all employees are united in a shared attempt to expand customers' perceptions as far as they can go.

The inner ring represents the sense of value that derives from businesses that meet their customers' most basic requirements, and nothing more. Those examples listed above—correct shipments, products that work as they're supposed to, accurate billing—are "inner ring" issues: they relate to customers' basic requirements. Any business that consistently fails to deliver value at least at the inner-ring level is a business whose very survival is in jeopardy. Where not even basic requirements are being met, there can be no perception of value whatsoever.

The expanded second ring represents the perception of value that results when *expectations*, too, are met. Expectations are not the same thing as requirements. Where a requirement falls into the need-to-have category, expectations tend to represent more of a *nice*-to-have proposition. Granted, failure to meet expectations also leads to disappointment, but usually not quite at the catastrophic deal-breaker level. Where customers tend to spell out their requirements in great detail ahead of time, they'll often leave their expectations unspoken, as if they were a given. (Spoken to a hotel reservation agent: "I need a nonsmoking room for next Thursday." [Unspoken: I

---

* Over the years this simple model has appeared in training programs distributed around the world by the Achieve Group, Zenger-Miller, and Times Mirror Training. Today it's a key conceptual component in Novations' *Customer Service From The Inside Out* program.

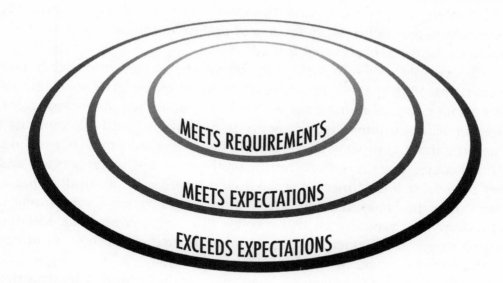

MEETS REQUIREMENTS

MEETS EXPECTATIONS

EXCEEDS EXPECTATIONS

expect it to have linen on the bed, running hot and cold water, a lock on the door, etc., etc.]) When all requirements *and* expectations are met, the customer's perception of value expands to the second ring. By definition, this is a satisfied customer, one who would be prepared to return. The larger the number of unmet expectations, however, the greater the sense of disappointment—and the more the customer's perception of value shrinks back down toward the inner-ring level.

The third ring represents the perception of value expanded as far outward as it can go. It's what results when, in addition to all customer requirements and expectations being met, at least some expectations are exceeded. It's where the "wow factor" creates an experience characterized not just by customer satisfaction, but by out-and-out *delight*. Customers of such businesses are not simply "prepared" to return, they often can't *wait* to return, and to bring friends and family along with them. (As an aside, even though it's cute to speak of "giving 110%" of oneself to something, giving 100% of oneself is of course all that's arithmetically possible. Similarly, adding further "wows" does not create a fourth ring in this construct—it simply further expands the third ring, until its dimensions encompass the whole planet, all of our solar system, the Milky Way Galaxy in its entirety.)

For all its deceptive simplicity, this three-ring model equips everyone in a business to grasp some fairly subtle and profound ironies—especially with regard to the quest for competitive advantage.

For example, everyone who understands the model immediately also understands that in their organization (as in all others), the great bulk of "the regular cost of doing business" is directed toward inner-ring issues. Meeting basic customer requirements is a full-time, costly, complicated enterprise that ties up most of the organization's resources most of the time. (And of course, any third-ring "frosting on the cake" enhancements will add very little value if the inner-ring cake itself is terrible.) Yet ironically, vital as basic inner-ring objectives may be for any organization's very survival, achieving them typically yields no competitive advantage at all. Meeting basic customer requirements is the minimum price every business must pay for the right to remain in operation for one more day—and that right is all it gives them. However huge their investment in the inner ring may be, this investment buys them no differentiation in the marketplace whatsoever.

Even consistently expanding the perception of value to the second ring, meeting all customer expectations, producing an army of fully satisfied customers—a daunting prospect for any business—even this produces very little in the way of competitive advantage. The inescapable reality is that virtually every other business is striving to do precisely the same, with equal determination. And not only do many succeed, some even manage to go beyond this and routinely expand their customers' perceptions into the third ring, into the realm of wow-factor delight. We refer to these mavericks as flashpoint businesses. By raising customer expectations generally, they make waves that continually threaten to swamp everybody else struggling to stay afloat.

It is indeed in the outer ring that the Wars for Competitive Advantage are waged. This is where flashpoint businesses continually deliver little extras their customers don't expect—or in the case of repeat business, things the returning customers certainly wouldn't expect to receive from competitors. On the battlefield of competitive business, the rules are starkly simple: whoever delivers the greatest overall perception of value wins.

An understanding of the three-ring model makes it easier for everyone to appreciate the greatest irony of all: those third-ring enhancements to the customer experience often cost next to nothing—in the case of friendly smiles or a courteous manner, their cost is *literally* nothing—yet they're typically what buys these businesses their greatest competitive advantage. A staggering bargain. Mighty business empires that operate in gigantic facilities and pay wages to thousands of workers can be crushed out of existence by a rival that better understands the power of those seemingly trivial third-ring elements to attract and retain customers.

The model can also be used to clarify why continuous improvement is important. Any wow-factor enhancement that exceeds expectations when first experienced by a customer will be *expected* by that customer from that point forward. Each third-ring enhancement thus immediately begins migrating inward toward the second ring, where expectations are merely met. The competitive advantage that derives from third-ring initiatives is powerful, but *temporary*. (The situation is compounded by the fact that once a business introduces a popular third-ring enhancement, it's usually only a matter of time before competitors find a way to replicate it in some form in their own setting.) For any organization to retain its competitive advantage, its workers need to be adding new third-ring innovations on a regular basis—which is the reason behind the *multiple* employee brainstorming sessions referred to in earlier chapters.

Yet another lesson the three-ring model helps everyone understand: why employee involvement and ownership is so absolutely vital. In any organization, who normally makes the decisions that affect inner-ring issues around basic products and services? The inner ring is a *management* domain, pure and simple. By comparison, who determines what happens, and how, in the outer ring—the ring with the greatest impact on competitive advantage? This is where frontline employees live and breathe. It is their tone of voice on the telephone, their smiles or scowls at the service counter, their attentiveness or disinterest throughout the transaction, that *control* how customers will perceive the organization as a whole. The employees already own the third ring, whether we like to acknowledge it or not. This is why we need to make very certain they feel a sense of personal involvement and ownership in it.

The model also helps businesses more clearly understand how transforming their cultures to expand customer perceptions into the outer ring requires improving quality and efficiency within the inner ring. (Such improvements, while they invariably lead to dramatic cost reductions at the operational level, are outside the scope of this book.)

As stated above, to track progress toward cultural alignment from the customer side of things, our measures will focus on the third ring—the primary source of competitive advantage, and the primary source of positive customer feedback to fuel employee motivation.

Professional Customers

The previous chapter expounds on getting those employees who come up with—and subsequently implement—their own third-ring ideas to personally collect feedback about these ideas directly from customers. But such feedback will therefore be limited to those newer aspects of the customer experience in particular. To measure *overall* customer perceptions, a measuring tool with a broader range is called for.

Does this mean another survey, a *customer* survey this time?

Customer surveys are not without their uses. But once again, they tend to generate a single "snapshot in time." Our interest in these pages is to measure *progress*, movement—and this requires the repeatability factor, so meaningful comparisons can be made. For many businesses, an attempt to administer the same survey to the same customers at regular intervals over the same period of time would entail formidable complications.

If it's too difficult to orchestrate repeatability with a random cross-section of customers, how about enlisting the services of a single, well-trained professional customer who can surreptitiously visit the same location(s) on a regular basis and assess predetermined aspects of the total customer experience, and report on these in a meaningful way?

Just mention "mystery shopper" or "secret shopper" in some organizations, and workers' blood pressure immediately shoots sky-high. The concept has the worst elements of "snoopervision" associated with it. It feels like entrapment, surveillance, Big Brother, the ultimate expression of management mistrust—and a major intensifier of employee cynicism and resentment. It carries these ugly associations because, alas, of how it has most often been used in the past.

The big difference in flashpoint businesses is that measurement in general (and mystery shopping in particular) is used not to expose villains, for the assignment of blame—but to expose heroes, for the assignment of recognition. It doesn't take long for employees' fears about mystery shopping to be allayed, once they can observe for themselves how it's being consistently used to uncover opportunities for celebration, rather than in any punitive way.

"I do think that [mystery shopping] tends to be a really good barometer, if you're careful," says Cheryl Beall, whose consulting firm provides mystery shoppers to major retail companies. "I actually will not work with clients that want to use it as some great disciplinary conk-you-on-the-head kind of thing. I always say, 'We need to discuss, before we do this, how this information will be used and what the outcomes and next steps will be.' You really have to be very careful about how you compile your questionnaire, the kind of people you're sending in, making sure that it tends to create a situation that's actually going to glean the right kind of information. I use mystery shopping basically as a diagnostic tool. It sets a benchmark, and then you identify training opportunities as a result."[5]

Mystery shopping is an important part of DNC's *GuestPath* program. "They go in and visit a property," Stewart Collins explains, "and then produce a report. Usually in any of our properties there's in the neighborhood of three thousand touch points that they measure. At the end of their evaluation they produce this report, and it boils it down to a summary page. We just had that assessment completed at Yosemite across six separate operating units, for hotels, retail, and transportation.

"Here's just an example," Stewart says, showing me a printout. "So this was October, 2006." He indicates one area on the sheet, and then moves to another. "This is June 2006. We do each of the properties twice a year. We may move to three times a year, because it's really powerful. So this is for the manager of [one of the hotels at Yosemite National Park]. She, like many strong managers, is competitive, and wants her score to go up. All of the managers in Yosemite are like that. Driven. So by showing these results side-by-side, there's no argument. This is an outside independent person [who] comes in, does an assessment that's very tactical. It's about our standards, and they're either yes or no. You either folded the folio into thirds, or you didn't. Two points or no points. Done. End of story."

This, Stewart points out, is different from the e-survey, which deals more in subjective customer opinions. "[The mystery shopper report] is broken down into four sections," he continues. "Guest Experience, Cleanliness, Conditions, Product Standards. If you look here, in the Guest Experience, there was the potential to get 166 points, and they got 142 of them. So their score came out as an 86%, up from 83%. So we're going through our evaluation, our wrap-up session, and we say, 'Okay, you went from an 83 to an 86. You should be celebrating. Three points is big. *Big*. But then, when you look at the detail, you look at the dining experience, it went from 80 to 89. *Phenomenal.* Unfortunately the hotel went from 87 to 79. So while the big picture shows growth, when you look at the detail there's pluses and minuses, as you would expect.

"So we do this wrap-up and we hand these out to the managers, and our vendor [of mystery shopping services] comes in and does their presentation, and the vice-president of operations doesn't really need to do a whole lot of jumping up and down screaming 'How come it went from 87 to 79,' because the manager is very competitive. [She] looks at the score, initially goes, 'Yeah! *Woo-hooo!*' then, 'Oh-oh. What happened? We dropped the ball. Somewhere along the line something happened.' So she can keep diving in and finding out what the situation was, and then come back with an explanation of why it is where it is."

This is of course right about where the conk-you-on-the-head part (to use Cheryl Beall's phrase) would be expected to kick in. "But in my role," says Stewart, "I fight hard for the management teams not to use this punitively. Let's use this in as positive a fashion as possible, let's dive in and find out where the hole is, and then try to close the gap." He alludes to the *GuestPath* program's continuous improvement cycle: "We created the standards; we train to the standards; we measure the standards; we [give] rewards and recognition; and then we train to the gaps. That really is the model that we use."

He points out the progress indicated by the multiple overall scores for this one hotel over time: "It went from 71.2, to 76.4, to 85.7, and then maintained the 85.7 on their October visit. Very powerful. From a motivational standpoint, provided you have a manager who's connected, cares, and has some passion for excellence, these are tremendously motivational."

Stewart next zeroes in on one of the sub-measures: "So now you go to 'cleanliness,'" he says. "Cleanliness in the hotel business is housekeeping manager, or executive housekeeper, or whatever it is. So you look at the number of points. 786 potential points, our vendor goes in and inspects 10 rooms, in detail. They got 742 points, which is a 94%—very, very positive. Going back to [the hotel in question] over the course of time, they started at 84, went to 86, went to 95, and they're at 94. They probably got to what I call a tipping point, where they're going to go up and down a point or two, [but] that's probably [all] their property can handle without spending two million dollars, and maybe [even then] only go to 96. But think about that over the course of time, when they started back in March of 2005. So you've seen this growth.

"So the general manager takes it to the executive housekeeper and shows it to her. She's in this case pretty ecstatic. And then [the general manager] takes it to her individual areas—the dining room manager, catering manager, various submanagers, and shows them that this has been growth. And provided it's supported and not used in that punitive way, it's very powerful [as it] moves through."

He begins really warming to his subject. "So these scores—this was done on Wednesday—were posted on Thursday in the employee break rooms. They were talked about in all the lineup meetings. That information was pushed down to the associates, so they could see, 'Hey, we did a good job.' And it's celebrated. [He points to one of the items on the chart that bears the improvement cycle]: Rewards and Recognition. Right now, in Yosemite, they're celebrating in all five properties. All five properties, in their big scores, went up. Now there's a couple of units that went down, but today it's celebrating. I think there [are] parties or receptions at all five properties today, because the scores came out yesterday. It's either today or tomorrow. And they're celebrating, they're having cake. And the managers of each of those properties [are] walking around today personally shaking people's hands, saying, 'Thank you for getting us to these scores.' Honestly, Yosemite knocked it out of the park this week. They did well. Very powerful."

"Now come Monday, there will be some discussions about training to the gaps, because we had some drops. So what happened? They'll have to go through the thick report to weed down to what is the problem. At [the hotel discussed earlier] we know what happened, we know that we lost the front office rooms manager, and we lost a couple of front desk clerks, so there [are] a couple of new people in there providing great friendly warm service, guests are happy, but not hitting the tactical things that we have to close the gap—the tactical standards. So they lost some points."

"In retail, they too knocked it out of the park, across the board. [Reading a succession of comparative scores]: "73 to 80, 81 to 89, 76 to 81, overall score 76 to 82, universal service standards from 82 to 89."

He pauses for a moment, to study one measure in particular—and then provides a striking example of how the numbers can yield information that might otherwise remain forever hidden. "But when you look through here," he says, "there's one [retail] property that embarrassed the manager, because they didn't perform where they should have. They went from a 67, which is barely acceptable to begin with, and they dropped to a 44. This was the universal service standards, so this is being in uniform, smiling, greeting the guest, looking up, using the guest's name—really basic [*GuestPath*] standards. And to be at 44%, honestly, we need to be thinking either we did a terrible job of training this person, or they are not buying into the program.

"In this situation we have an associate who works extremely well while being watched and clearly doesn't do that when he's not being watched. So it might be an okay associate in the wrong environment, because this is a pretty independent store, you're by yourself a lot. The manager came to this associate's defense and said, 'He performs fantastic every time *I'm* there!'"

Stewart makes a notation on the printout for his own reference and then pushes it aside. "We're not going to attack that today," he says. "That's Monday. Today they all need to be celebrating. The vice-president of operations is having a cocktail party at her house, because [the scores for] five properties went up for [the] four last [mystery] shops, and that [kind of thing] just doesn't happen in our industry."[6]

Not every business has pockets deep enough to permit mystery shopping on such a scale, of course. But the principles involved apply at *any* scale. You want someone who knows what they're supposed to be looking for, who behaves like a perfectly typical customer, and who assigns numerical values to various aspects of the total experience. Later, this same person (or another with an equal grasp of what's to be observed and evaluated) can return and repeat the process at regular intervals. The comparative scores depict improvement—progress—or the lack of it.

A key "job requirement" for any mystery shopper is *impartiality*. Anyone with potential social or family ties to existing employees should be disqualified. An ex-employee—even one with a superb performance record—may seem an attractive choice, because he or she "already knows the business." Worst possible choice. Not only will some old ties almost certainly be revived ("Hey, what brings *you* here?"), such an individual may also have a lingering axe to grind with one or more coworkers or managers. Your ideal candidate is a professional mystery shopper from out of town who knows nothing about your operation—but has experience in evaluating businesses of the same type as yours. (Industry associations are a good source of recommendations.) Failing that: someone from out of town who is not acquainted with a single one of your employees, and who sincerely wants to help you derive an accurate and impartial picture of what your customers experience.

But just what exactly are the specific kinds of things this mystery shopper is supposed to be looking for?

Evaluating the Total Customer Experience

The first step in our four-step culture-change process, you'll recall, involves getting employees involved in coming up with their own ideas for improving the customer experience. In three-ring terms, this level of involvement represents formally giving them ownership of the third ring—which they've always controlled anyway, though typically not with any great sense of personal pride attached to it. In the previous chapter we intro-duced three Customer Focus Principles, which serve as the basis for three rounds of creative employee brainstorming (as outlined in the "facilitator's guide" that is *Customer Service Made Easy*). These same three Customer Focus Principles also provide the perfect framework for defining what mys-tery shoppers should be evaluating.

1. Exceed the Customer's Expectations Every Step of the Way

During their brainstorming sessions, employees break a typical customer transaction down into its constituent chronological steps. They then gen-erate ideas for exceeding expectations (that is, adding a third-ring element) to each step in turn.

Your mystery shopper should therefore be provided with the same list of steps the brainstorming employees identified in their session. Assigned to each step is a numerical scale that allows the shopper to assign a score. The score indicates the extent to which the shopper's expectations were exceeded (or not) in each step.

2. Make the Customer Feel Important

In their brainstorming sessions, employees next revisit each step in the transaction sequence and look for ways to make customers feel more wel-come, valued, and important. (They also look for things to eliminate from the customer experience, to avoid making customers feel the opposite.)

On your mystery shopper's list of steps in the transaction, each step should be assigned a *second* numerical scale. This one records a score that reflects how important (or not) the shopper was made to feel in each step of the transaction.

3. Tailor the Experience to Fit the Customer

In the final round of employee brainstorming, participants identify major cus-tomer categories, and any unique expectations each of these categories may have. Their objective is to generate ideas for meeting (or preferably, exceeding) those unique expectations that apply only to specific categories of customers.

Your mystery shopper should therefore be provided with the same list of major customer categories the brainstorming employees came up with, with each category assigned a numerical scale. The shopper looks for indicators that each of these customer categories in particular is being accommodated in some way and scores accordingly.

This three-element framework produces a relatively simple tool any mystery shopper can use at regular intervals to evaluate the effect employee involvement and ownership of the third ring is having on the customer experience. It would naturally make sense to provide your mystery shopper (who may not be acquainted with the structure of the brainstorming process) some preliminary explanation of the process and its goals.

Also, over a longer period of time, employees may brainstorm other *kinds* of transactions, which would yield a different list of steps. They may also think of new or different categories of customers, which would again affect the mystery shopper's list. In every case, that which is being measured should always represent a perfect mirror image of that which the employees are trying to accomplish. How else can progress in these specific areas be confirmed?

Our goal is a highly motivated workforce. Because lack of cultural alignment destroys motivation, this book has devoted various chapters to each of six separate elements of organizational culture. We refer to the six as "flashpoint factors" because the flashpoint effect represents cultural alignment in its purest form—and the flashpoint effect cannot be sustained *unless* all six are in alignment. In this chapter we've focused on two aspects of measurement, related to the two components of the flashpoint effect: employee motivation and customer satisfaction.

What none of the foregoing indicates, however, is how in real-world terms these six flashpoint factors all tend to overlap and blend together into a single cultural whole. We separate them out on the written page so that we can more easily appreciate what each one represents, and how we might go about making any necessary changes to each. But inevitably, changes to any one affect all the others to at least some degree—and often to a great degree.

For example, Chapter 4 suggests that "... the role of internal communication becomes to publicize hero stories of workers doing useful and necessary things for customers ..." The logical question becomes, where's this steady flow of hero stories to come from? The logical answer is, from customer feedback collected by the employees themselves (as described in Chapter 5), and from data and any anecdotal support material supplied by mystery shoppers, as outlined in this chapter. (Another obvious source would be any existing surveys or other mechanisms through which your organization already collects customer feedback on a regular basis.) In "flashpoint factor" terms, we can say that both CUSTOMER DELIGHT and MEAS-UREMENT feed INTERNAL COMMUNICATION.

And as we're about to see, they feed RECOGNITION even more directly.

Notes

1. Stewart Collins, DNC, interview with the author, October 31, 2006.
2. Cathi Rittelmann, Novations Group, interview with the author, January 16, 2007.
3. Ibid.
4. Mark Emmitte, Stage Stores, interview with the author, December 5, 2006.
5. Cheryl Beall, Retail 101, interview with the author, October 20, 2006.
6. Stewart Collins, DNC, interview with the author, November 3, 2006.

Chapter 7

Right and Wrong Ways to Celebrate Successes

earlier clash between the celebrity and photographers at the party. No injuries were reported.

"Too Many Award Shows" Wins Best Documentary Award

HOLLYWOOD—The controversial hour-long documentary *Are There Too Many Award Shows On TV?* took top honors in the documentary category at last night's first annual "Tappie" Awards show, broadcast live from Los Angeles.

"I didn't think we had a chance," said producer Serge Desrosiers, accepting the award.

The Tappie Awards, named after the Institute of Television Award Programs (ITAP), honor top achievements in such categories as "best opening production number" and "shortest acceptance speech." There's already buzz that producer Desrosiers' speech will be nominated for this latter award at next year's show.

Producers of the weekday entertainment program *Showbiz Headlines* devoted a ten-minute segment to Desrosiers' unexpected win. The show's executive producer hopes industry insiders will remember the piece when the Seggie Award nominations are announced in the fall. Seggie Awards recognize outstanding segments on entertainment news-magazine programs.

The actual Tappie Award, a gold-plated figure clutching a small statuette-sized version of itself, is favored to win an "Ada" for best trophy design at next month's annual Award Design Awards ceremony. Last year's Ada telecast was crowned "best award show of the year" during the closing

W hat makes TV award shows so popular? Some might argue it's the fascination people have with celebrities—these shows give viewers glimpses of a lot of them together in one place at one time. But many of these award shows are preceded by "red-carpet" interview shows and are followed by post-awards-party interview shows—programs in which viewers get to see and hear even more of the same celebrities. Why then are the TV ratings for these pre- and post-interview programs always much lower than for the awards ceremony itself? There may be something else at play here.

Typical comments heard after every award show: "I'm so glad _____ won. I *like* him." "I thought for sure _____ was finally going to win one this year." "I felt really bad for _____ when she didn't get it." It's worth taking a moment to analyze sentiments like these. They represent more than just neutral curiosity about who will win—they reflect a genuine *hope* that certain individuals will receive the recognition they deserve for their good work.

Let's take a quick look at some real-life examples of extremely successful "celebration events" from a variety of business settings. In particular, we're looking for any characteristics they have in common with each other, and with popular TV award ceremonies.

"We receive some heart-wrenching letters from our customers," Pamela Miller once told me during an interview for an earlier book. At the time she was vice president of strategic planning at Blue Cross Blue Shield of New Jersey. "Someone may write in and say something like, 'Maureen is really fabulous. My child is dying of leukemia, and I had half a million dollars in claims, and Maureen spent a whole day with me going through everything and helping me figure it all out. She's the greatest,' that kind of thing. We'll arrange to take a picture of the customer and publish excerpts from the letter and stuff it into the payroll envelopes for everybody in the company to see."

She then described an unusual annual event. "Once a year we invite 150 customers to lunch. And we give them a chance to present flowers or a gift (which we pay for) to the person they wrote about. They meet each other face to face. It's very emotional. Very emotional. Last year it was unbelievable. We had a retired fighter pilot and he just spontaneously got up and talked about how if there were more people in the world like our employees the world would be such a better place. On his own he brought two dozen roses for this one woman employee and presented them to her. People were crying. It was unbelievable. These lunches are standing room only. We do it once a year, and we get so many beautiful letters it's hard to decide who to invite."[1]

Every year the CVS/pharmacy chain sends a video production team out to meet customers and families of "Paragons"—store managers or pharmacists who delivered an exceptional customer experience during the year. The video team creates a mini-documentary that looks and sounds like a network news report, chronicling how these Paragons (typically around 15 in number) have made a difference in customers' lives. The video documentaries are screened at the annual corporate sales meeting, with some 25 hundred managers in attendance, as part of an extravagant Paragon Awards presentation. "We fly [the winners] to the meeting," says Eileen Howard Dunn, vice president of corporate communications and community relations. "They're acknowledged by their colleagues.... It's their night to shine.... They're all given awards and then they have their videos that are shown. It's a *huge* deal.... Everybody wants to be a Paragon.... My production director [spends] three or four months on the project every year."[2]

"We last year had the top awards in the company, the Legacy of Service Awards," says DNC's Stewart Collins. "The event was in Walt Disney World in Florida. We flew the top associates that won this award to Florida for a week, put them up, gave them side trips, and [it] culminated in this award banquet in front of all of the general managers from all of the divisions, and some assorted other dignitaries.... They were presented the award by the chairman. And [ours is a] privately held, multibillion dollar company. [The chairman] handing a gal at the sports arena—who pushes a popcorn cart or whatever—he hands her this award, shakes her hand.... They tell the story, they show the picture up on the wall, and all the general managers' standing ovation—very moving. Very moving."[3]

Here's an example that derives neither from business settings nor from the entertainment industry. During television coverage of the Olympic Games, time is always taken to include shots of the gold-medal winners standing on the platform as the appropriate national anthem plays in the background. No special athletic ability is required to stand motionless listening to music—so why bother including such scenes? It's the winners' facial expressions, the tears welling in their eyes, that often make these scenes the most memorable part of the experience for viewers at home (who sometimes feel a little lump forming in their own throats as well).

Applause, recognition, emotion. These are key elements of every award ceremony, every wedding anniversary party, every post-game victory celebration, every retirement party—every situation humans can dream up to acknowledge the achievements of other humans in some way. As mentioned in our Chapter 5 discussion around customer feedback, it isn't only those on the *receiving* end of applause that feel good. Television viewers sitting in extremely modest homes, living extremely modest lives, nevertheless feel a sense of personal satisfaction when good work done by someone wealthy and famous—someone who seemingly already has it all—is acknowledged in a big splashy ceremony that moves the recipient to tears.

When the award recipient happens to be someone we actually know, someone we *work with*, that sense of satisfaction can become even more intense. "People were crying," said Pamela Miller (above) in the plural, even though at that moment only one customer was honoring only one employee. When Wayne Charness (senior vice-president of corporate communications at Hasbro Toys) described an all-employee meeting in which a guest speaker thanked workers for their charitable donations of toys to underprivileged children, he used a familiar phrase: "There wasn't a dry eye in the house."[4] (I was struck to see his own eyes misting over as he recalled the event.) When Pam Miller used the phrase "Very emotional," she emphasized it by saying it twice. When Stewart Collins used the phrase "Very moving," he *also* said it twice for emphasis.

What makes TV award shows so popular is that people love seeing others receive positive recognition for what they've accomplished. *People love cheering for winners and for heroes.* When the honorees are visibly moved by the ovation, the cheering crowd is often moved in turn—another chain reaction of contagious emotion, deeply satisfying for everyone involved.

It's a form of collective satisfaction many workers in many organizations seldom get to experience on the job. Even when good work is acknowledged, it's often handled in private, one-on-one, with an absolute minimum of public fanfare. Still a nice thing for the individual recipient, of course—but no one else gets to participate. There's no collective cheering to amplify the immediate impact and emotion.

If our approach to motivation is one that emphasizes involvement for all employees, our approach to recognition must mirror this. Virtually without exception, flashpoint cultures are also cultures of near-constant celebration—with as many employees involved as possible.

The Hidden Mirror

In many simple optical illusions, the image tends to vacillate before our eyes. One moment it looks like one thing, a moment later it "flips" and becomes something else. Is this a dark goblet, or two white mirror-image faces in profile, nose-to-nose?

At first some people may have trouble seeing the faces. The dark goblet naturally dominates as a foreground object on a white background. But then once you do manage to flip it and see the faces as white-foreground-objects-on-a-dark-background, you never really lose them again. Even when you try to go back to seeing only a goblet, the faces keep intruding. The same people who at first had trouble seeing the faces will sometimes later be astounded the faces are not immediately obvious to others.

The Big Disconnect, the invisible killer of businesses described in Chapter 5, is deadly precisely because it remains invisible to its victims. Those businesses that do not *see* the connection between customer satisfaction and employee motivation are typically unaware that they're missing something others consider as obvious as the two noses on the two faces above. Once a business culture has experienced its collective "aha!" and can see both aspects of the reality before it, and how they're related, the connection becomes obvious and unavoidable. The same managers who at first had trouble seeing the connection will sometimes later be astounded that it's not immediately obvious to others.

For the goblet illusion to work, the two faces must of course be perfect mirror-images of each other. Part of the reality that remains invisible to those afflicted with the big disconnect is another kind of mirror-image: EMPLOYEE MOTIVATION AND CUSTOMER SATISFACTION ARE ALWAYS MIRROR-IMAGES OF EACH OTHER.

It's true within their particular business setting—even if they can't see it—because it's true in *all* business settings. Where employees are cynical and demoralized, no amount of customer service training, no amount of disciplinary action, no amount of managerial pressure is going to get them consistently delivering a delightful customer experience. In businesses where workers are crackling with energy and enthusiastic about achieving an objective they all believe in, customer delight is practically a given. Attempts to drive either side of the equation upward, while disregarding the other, have always been—and will always be—costly (and demoralizing) exercises in futility.

In the previous chapter we introduced the Three-Ring Model as a mechanism for understanding customers' perception of value. In keeping with the mirror-image theme, this same model helps clarify how *employees* perceive the business they work for as well.

Bumper sticker: *WORK SUCKS, BUT I NEED THE BUCKS*. Earning enough to live on is the inner-ring basic requirement of any job. Workers also have expectations, however, in terms of how they'll be treated by their employer. If their requirements and expectations are all met, the workers' perception of value expands out to the second ring—they become satisfied employees. Some businesses go beyond meeting the requirements and expectations of their employees and routinely *exceed* some expectations. This is where employees experience the "wow factor," where jobs become deeply meaningful and fulfilling for the delighted workers involved. These are businesses in which employees are motivated.

The accounts of "applause, recognition, and emotion" cited above are examples of businesses expanding workers' perception of value into the third ring. These organizations do this in parallel with their employees' efforts to expand *customers'* perceptions into the third ring. It's the mirror-image aspect—obvious to them, invisible to others—that is absolutely critical if the chain reaction effect is to kick in.

The recruitment ads may continue to seek job candidates who are "self-motivated," but businesses in alignment place the basic responsibility for employee motivation elsewhere. DNC's Stewart Collins makes no bones about it: "It's the responsibility of the manager to help that person ... have satisfaction in their job.... The associate needs to feel that he or she has a voice, that they fit in, that they're important, that what they do is valued."[5]

Shortly, in this chapter, we're going to identify four attributes that give celebrations of business success their greatest motivational impact.

Too Much of a Good Thing?

I generally like to avoid being impolite. For example, if over lunch a manager were to say to me, "Isn't there a danger of overdoing this whole recognition thing?" I would try to avoid doing a "spit-take" and spraying my mouthful of cola all over his or her expensive suit. Spit-takes are just plain impolite.

It's almost always those businesses doling out the least recognition that worry most about dangers associated with doling out too much of it. The standard concern is that something that is prized because it's rare will lose all of its perceived value if it becomes an ordinary everyday experience. And this might very well hold true—for things that are prized because they're rare. Employees prize recognition, however, for a different reason altogether.

As you read this book on employee motivation, do you grow concerned that the process outlined herein may work *too* well for you? Afraid your operating costs and employee turnover rates may sink too low? Developing any nagging concerns that your business may become *overly* profitable?

Intriguingly, those who speak of "too much of a good thing" seldom complain about too much of *these* good things.

Ever notice how fish do not seem bothered by constant dampness? They don't seem to mind being soaking wet all day long, throughout their entire lives. Give them a chance to dry off a bit in the warm sunlight, and they waste no time making quite a fuss about getting right back into the wetness without delay. Humans feel much the same way about air. They breathe the same stuff in, day in, day out—wouldn't you think it'd be starting to get a bit monotonous by now? But cut off their supply for even just a few moments, and they immediately drop everything else and begin pursuing their beloved air with impressive single-mindedness.

There are things in life that many people find enjoyable, yet are not essential for survival. Hot-fudge sundaes come to mind. Too much of these kinds of things may prove harmful in the long run. But no fish has ever suffered ill effects from access to too much clean water, nor people from access to too much fresh air. The danger of "too much of a good thing" doesn't always apply to survival essentials.

Employee enthusiasm is a survival issue in any business. In those that have developed a flashpoint culture, *high* levels of employee enthusiasm are absolutely essential for the survival of that culture. Deprive the workers of their steady diet of recognition and celebration based on positive customer feedback, and the motivation level immediately begins to drop—with its counterpart, customer satisfaction, dropping in mirror-image parallel. The chain-reaction effect ends, and the work becomes just another dreary job to help pay the bills.

"How can you over-recognize somebody?" asks retail consultant Cheryl Beall. "I don't think it's possible. I want to meet the person that feels over-appreciated!"[6]

Where there *is* a danger of overdoing something, Cheryl believes, is in the use of traditional employee rewards, rather than recognition, as a prime motivator. "I find that [incentives] can be very much over-used," she says. "In fact, when I was at Bergdorf's years ago, we had vendors develop incentives all the time, and so Mont Blanc would come and [say], 'Okay, if you sell three Meisterstück [pens] then you get a Meisterstück.' And then the linens person would come and [say], 'If you sell three sheet sets then you get something.' And I was standing on the floor speaking to the floor manager one day when an employee came up and said to their manager, 'I just sold a whatever—do I get something for that?' And I just—" Cheryl pauses, as if to catch herself before a profanity passes her lips. "And I said, 'Yes, actually, I think it's called *commission*.' I was really fried about it." Incentives of this kind, she believes, work *against* cultural alignment, by reinforcing self-interest. "[The associates] are not doing it because it's the right thing for the customer, they're doing it because 'I'm going to get a prize.'"[7]

What's the big motivator at Lindt & Sprüngli? "It's recognition," says Brian Gallagher. More than money? "*Way* more than money." He describes his company as one that pays "very middle-of-the-road," but as he emphasizes, this has no adverse effect on employee retention or the quality of the work. "I can look at a million other companies who—they pay the money, but they're turning managers every 18 to 24 months. [Lindt & Sprüngli's turnover rate] is probably 20 percent lower than the industry average.... You cannot attribute it to money. There's always somebody who's going to pay you a dollar more—and I'll tell you, in my experience, when we hire people for a dollar more, you don't get it from them!" Does his experience suggest there are more effective ways to draw the best out of workers? "Absolutely."[8]

"Recognition carries a lot more weight than rewards," DNC's Stewart Collins agrees. "There's a gentleman that I worked with in Yosemite, Sean Costello, who was the manager of rentals. He's been in the park for 24 years, loves the park, went there on a spur-of-the-moment trip, has never left—met his wife there, has raised his family there, absolutely loves Yosemite. And he epitomized, to me, the sense of *GuestPath*. We were at the little Badger Pass ski area, great little ski area, and Sean was the manager who, in the morning, before the rental shop opened, had a team huddle with his associates. Honestly, they have kind of an ugly job, not terribly rewarding job. He would have a team huddle, he would sing *Happy Birthday* to the appropriate person in the room, he thanked all of them first thing in the morning, for coming in to work. *Every day!* He made [the associates] a team—they bowled together, they would have a pizza party together—but the most powerful aspect was that personal thanking you for coming to work. Now it's eight o'clock in the morning, it's 10 degrees outside, they've ridden on the bus for an hour and a half to get there . . . and he takes that time to thank them for coming to work. And that was very powerful. Then, he would go out and greet the guests and thank *them* for coming. At the end of the day, he would be out on the snow, literally yelling, 'Thanks for coming! We hope to see you again tomorrow!' *To the guests!* Then he'd close the shop by going and thanking every single one of the associates: 'Thanks for coming in today, you did a great job.' Whether they did a great job or not, 'Thanks for coming in, you did a great job.' And you know, he had less absenteeism, he had less turnover, he had people doing a pretty [unpleasant] job, fitting boots, smelling people's feet, not great. People wanted to work with him, because of that *recognition* that took place. I think that that's much more powerful than the rewards."[9]

Businesses that have learned to see the power of recognition to promote cultural alignment typically don't lose a lot of sleep worrying that they may be dispensing "too much" of it.

The Four Attributes of Motivational Celebration

Aside from the *quantity* of recognition businesses provide, there's also the *quality* aspect to consider. Not all efforts to celebrate successes are equally effective, in terms of their motivational impact. Those celebrations that deliver the biggest motivational punch typically share four attributes.

1. The Effort Quotient

Throughout the previous chapters, positive customer feedback has been touted as the most powerful employee motivator of all. Nevertheless, "To please your boss is a powerful thing," says Brian Gallagher.

He offers an example. "If I'm a store manager, I may see a thousand different customers in a day. To get a thank-you from one of them, it's great, keeps me energized, makes me realize why I'm doing what I'm doing. But I'm motivated for a much longer period of time if I hear that same thing from somebody within my organization—my district manager, my regional manager, or somebody at the home office who is almost having to make an effort to recognize that, as opposed to a customer who's in the store regardless."[10]

Brian's observation warrants a moment's reflection. Clearly a generic second-ring "thank-you" from a satisfied customer would be expected to carry less motivational impact than a third-ring rave from a delighted customer referring to a specific innovation, especially when delivered directly to the worker(s) responsible for that particular innovation. But Brian also mentions the power of feedback from someone inside the organization who "is almost having to make an effort to recognize." This "effort" aspect is critical. It tends to be directly proportional to the motivational effect the recognition will have on the recipient(s).

This is similar to something many of us have experienced in our personal lives—the feeling that comes over us when we receive a gift or card that someone very clearly went to *a lot of trouble* to find or create or arrange just for our benefit. How strikingly different such a gift or card feels from one (even a fancy or expensive one) that feels not entirely appropriate somehow, and that seems to have been given very little thought, very little time, very little effort by the giver. A friend once told me of a family member who in the flurry of gift opening around the Christmas tree would always make the same pronouncement to all: "Remember, if you don't like the gifts I got you, you can always swap 'em among yourselves." According to my friend, this individual tended to openly admit the gifts all came from one store, and were all purchased at one time, often at the last possible moment. These "generic" gifts sometimes secretly went to the garbage unused, my friend admitted. It was a quiet gesture of personal protest—the gifts had become a source of resentment rather than a source of joy.

Low-effort rewards in the workplace can backfire in a similar way. "Prior to *GuestPath*," says Stewart Collins, "we had a very hit-or-miss consistency in rewarding, we weren't terribly good at it."[11] Camille Maxwell describes a reward scheme that predated the *GuestPath* program. "[The former managers] used to give out a piece of paper with, like, 'Yosemite Bucks,'" she says, "and [employees could use them to] purchase things out of the incentive cabinet. Well the incentive cabinet, there was nothing in it! [Everybody] used to call it 'the cabinet of shame.' Somebody would give you employee bucks so that you could purchase from a cabinet that's literally empty, there's nothing in there. It's like Charlie Brown trick-or-treating, [he] got rocks, it was just rocks. Eventually [managers] would fill up the cabinet, and what they would do is they would purchase what seemed like just enough so that people [would] use up all their bucks, and then it'd empty up the cabinet again." Did employees at the time value these bits of paper? "I lost my bucks!" Camille replies with a laugh. "I don't even know where they are!"[12]

As the degree of effort invested in the "thank-you" visibly shrinks before workers' eyes, so too does its motivational effect. When recognition is handled as a mechanized low-priority afterthought, it can begin to have a less-than-zero *negative* effect, becoming fuel for cynicism.

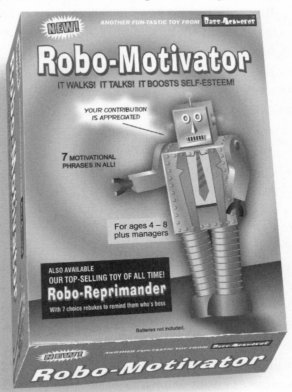

"What we really worked hard with *GuestPath*," says Stewart Collins, "was to create that celebration, where you don't just reward, there's a celebration attached to it."13

The elaborately-staged celebration events cited at the beginning of this chapter all represent examples of management teams going to a *tremendous* amount of trouble to give something meaningful to their workers. The magnitude of the organization's effort is plainly visible to all. Everyone knows events on such a scale entail extensive planning and organizing, not to mention cost. The core message remains "thank you for a job well done"—but the mechanism for *delivering* the message becomes awe-inspiring to everyone involved. It's especially awe-inspiring to the honorees themselves.

Energized businesses instinctively (or perhaps very deliberately) avoid mechanized no-effort forms of recognition. As we're about to see, even when budget limitations preclude lavish extravaganzas on the scale of a TV awards show, management still invests time and thought into forms of recognition that are personalized and specific. They *go to the trouble* of making it meaningful for the recipients.

2. The Internal/External Meld

Beyond their effort quotient, big splashy recognition events like those described at the beginning of this chapter have a second characteristic in common. They all use customer feedback as the basis for their awards. The event is organized and funded by (internal) management, but it's in celebration of feedback from (external) customers. Such an event is thus neither strictly "internal" nor "external" in origin. It represents a melding of the two—which makes it a clear and powerful reinforcer of cultural alignment. This is management making it possible for the whole organization to pause and celebrate movement in the *one single direction* that matters most to everyone.

Contrast this with a manager bestowing an award for the tidiest workspace, or best attendance record, or lowest number of forgotten cover sheets on the TPS Reports.* Recognition for such purely internal achievements reflects issues that may matter more to the manager than to the recipient—and will certainly matter very little to the other employees, and not at all to customers.

The melding of internal and external recognition retains its motivational power even on a small scale, provided there's also some visible "effort quotient" involved. Mark Emmitte describes how the Stage Stores home office receives complimentary letters from customers every day. "Ernie Cruse [executive vice president of store operations] sends every associate who received a compliment a personalized letter that is hand-signed by him," says Mark. "And it is amazing how many responses you get back from associates thanking him for sending them a letter. It really is amazing. It means a lot to them, and one of the things that we found out very recently ... where we were asking them about the things that were most important to them, they all said simple things like recognition, such as the one I described. It was not what we often expect." Would most managers have expected the workers to cite money as the most important thing to them? "Without question I would say that. [It's been] eye-opening.... The responses that you get from management when they hear [this is] what's important to associates are eye-opening, because it's almost with disbelief. And what that shows you is that some of the reasons why ... an individual manager may not be getting the results he or she wants is because they're approaching it from the wrong direction.... What [associates are] looking for are simple things in recognition and appreciation for work done. And it's so simple, so easy—and yet so forgotten."[14]

"Our positive customer letters have more than quadrupled," says Kate Spade's Beth Guastella, "and I'm not exaggerating, I bet there at least either two e-mails and/or hard notes that we get per week, where a customer has taken the time to write about a particular associate experience. Any time there is any sort of correspondence from a customer, number one, we respond to the customer immediately. Then what we'll do is, obviously the employee is cc'ed on the note back to the customer, as is their manager, as is HR, so that the employee sees that we really believe in this, and we're very happy about it, which we write about in the letter to the customer.

---

* The TPS cover sheet crisis will be familiar to fans of Mike Judge's 1999 comedy film *Office Space*, essential viewing for any serious student of employee motivation.

[The employees] see that we're very happy with this service level. Also ... when a letter comes in, then I'll write a personal note to the associate, thanking them for whatever specifically it was that they did that went above and beyond."[15]

In stressing how this form of internally delivered/externally triggered recognition conveys to recipients "that we really believe in this," Beth is acknowledging its function as an enhancer of cultural alignment.

3. The Hero Story

In each of the large-scale celebrations described at the start of the chapter, the centerpiece of the event is the story: what the honorees specifically did to help one or more specific customers in some remarkable way. These are the hero stories that are being recounted and celebrated—and hero stories have always had the power to entrance and move people. Most of the novels ever written, most of the films ever produced, most theatrical plays, most TV dramas, most fables and myths and legends, most fairy tales, most bedtime stories, are accounts of one or more individuals overcoming all obstacles to achieve something heroic. The love of a "good story" is a universal human trait going back to tales told around fires at the mouths of caves.

In Chapter 4 we described internal communication as a mechanism for reinforcing cultural alignment by showing employees a reflection of themselves "caught in the act of being 'useful and necessary in the world'" (Maslow's phrase). We can therefore use this same idea as the basis for a definition of "hero story" within the context of recognition in the workplace: a hero story is one that depicts employees being useful and necessary in the world.

"We used to own the three big riverboats on the Mississippi," says DNC's Stewart Collins. "The American Queen, Delta Queen, and Mississippi Queen—big paddlewheels on the river.... When New Orleans was devastated [by Hurricane Katrina in 2005] there were a lot of negative stories, but in [an internal communication document] we really kind of talked about how other people within our organization went to their help, and did that kind of thing."[16]

This is the sort of national-headlines tragedy that comes to mind when most people think about hero stories. But in business settings, the kinds of third-ring elements that wow customers would seldom make it into even the local headlines. Still, this fact does not minimize the impact these interactions have on the customers involved. Flashpoint businesses celebrate their "little" hero stories with big hoopla. It's worth noting, for example, that Stewart speaks in more detail and with more passion about the effect of his colleague's everyday recognition of good work in the ski area than he does about the efforts employees made to help victims of a one-time hurricane. (And as an aside, when I remarked to Stewart that in the near future he'll be able to present his colleague with a copy of this book and direct him to the passage in which he is mentioned, Stewart whispered under his breath, "That would be so fantastic. That would make me cry." Applause, recognition, emotion.)

An example of a little hero story from Beth Guastella: "A customer came in and was literally in tears, ... there was some personal tragedy that had occurred in her life. And she came into the store, and so the sales associates very much felt as though—and it was these two women [associates] in particular—that they had a greater responsibility than just selling a handbag or a pair of shoes, that they were actually helping this customer along. And this customer ended up staying in the store an hour and a half, and left, and turned and said to them, 'I feel so much better than when I first walked in this store. You two have made my day. I will always think about you and I will always think about Kate Spade.'" Once again, nothing in this to warrant a special TV news bulletin—but it deeply affected the customer, and the two women who helped her as well.

Note that this delighted customer's feedback was not in response to some innovative third-ring idea or project these employees had come up with and implemented ahead of time. The gathering of *that* kind of feedback is the subject matter of Chapter 5; in our culture-change process it is typically gathered by the workers themselves, who experience its motivational effect immediately. In this case the customer was expressing appreciation for how two associates helped her in a purely spontaneous *ad hoc* manner. Hero stories recounted in celebration events will often tend to reflect customer feedback of this second kind. It's often feedback customers provide to management, after the fact. (The workers may not even know about it until management discloses it as part of the celebration event.) Its motivational effect will therefore also typically be felt after the fact. Celebration events become "time-release motivators"—a powerful way to prolong the fourth step in our four-step culture-change process *("Use [customer] feedback as the basis for employee recognition")*. The more skillfully you apply the kinds of measurement tools outlined in the previous chapter, the more such feedback you'll likely have at your disposal to play with.

Note too that this kind of spontaneous customer-focused behavior on the part of employees virtually *never* happens in cultures full of cynicism and antagonism toward management. That's why it figures in the *final* step of our process—a certain level of alignment must be achieved (through the first three steps of the process) before employees will begin routinely delighting customers on their own initiative, in response to unanticipated opportunities as they arise.

Beth Guastella describes how she has seen the culture in her own organization evolve. "As [associates] develop relationships with customers," she says, "I think they personally get something out of it. I think they love feeling special from the customer—and they do.... Customers make them feel very special, and write them notes. In fact, it's evident at the holidays, when all these customers start bringing them gifts, whether it be plates of cookies or brownies or, you know, 'Oh girls, I know you're going to be busy so here's a tin of popcorn.' ... One store even had a customer bring a tin of lasagna!" How common is this sort of thing in Beth's experience? "Very common," she says. "But even when I was [in] my early days at Hermes, when I was a store manager, we had that happen there too.... Some of our stores, they have some customers who come in three time a week, just to say hi. Sometimes it's 'I'm in the mall, just wanted to come by and say hi.' Obviously when a customer does that, they're getting something out of this relationship other than a handbag and a pair of shoes and some jewelry. They're getting something out of it psychologically and/or emotionally, other than merchandise."

Beth relates how a customer recently became engaged to be married in one of her stores. "The fiancé came in and said, 'She loves you all,' and I guess he knew the team there very well, and he bought a bag [and hid] the ring in the bag, and he brought her in. The woman thought she was just coming in to shop, and literally the team all knew she was getting ready to get engaged, and she got engaged in the Kate Spade store.... This happened about two months ago.... [It] was the most incredible example of developing customer loyalty. The fact that a customer would choose to get engaged—obviously engagement and wedding is one of those momentous occasions in your life—and the fact that someone chose to do that in a Kate Spade store to me just spoke volumes."[17]

The closed-loop chain-reaction effect in action: when a business empowers its workers to look like heroes in customers' eyes, the mere loyal *return* of these customers becomes a motivational form of recognition and validation in and of itself. "I have regular customers that come in every single day, and they're happy and they say hi to me,... that's what makes me happy," says Tracy Brown (an employee at the busiest Dunkin' Donuts store in the world) in Chapter 1. The more management can celebrate specific examples of workers going the extra mile for such customers, the more motivational energy it can apply to the chain reaction, to keep it bubbling.

4. The Public Forum

The final attribute all the big award shows (and the business celebrations described at the start of the chapter) have in common: a large audience.

In a small-group setting, no matter how energetically the master of ceremonies shouts, "Come on! Let's *give it up* for Robin!"—if the total audience numbers three people, the clippety-clappety sound of their applause will inevitably be underwhelming. The more hands that can be heard clapping, the sweeter the effect. The more voices raised in cheering, the greater the motivational impact.

I have often had occasion to be on a long late-night flight, trying to snooze. I hate it when I discover the in-flight movie is to be a comedy. It means there won't be much snoozing in store for this sleepy traveler. Every few moments the quiet of the darkened cabin is shattered by loud cackles of laughter emanating from surrounding seats. Are these cacklers traveling together, I find myself wondering. Do they even know each other? More to the point—would they be cackling this loudly if they were at home, watching this same movie all by themselves? On the screen, the wedding cake winds up covering the face of the lead character. Apparently no one on my flight could see this coming. Apparently no one on my flight has ever seen a cake hit a character in the face in any movie or TV show prior to this flight. Sleepers be damned—this cake-in-the-face is so hilarious, it *demands* loud cackles.

What these cackling strangers prove (as do those strangers at sports events who collectively perform "the wave," for example) is that people sharing an experience as a single entity—as an audience—feel connected in a particular way. Even total strangers at a cocktail party who through casual conversation discover they were both in the audience at the same concert in the past, or at some other earlier public event, still immediately feel more connected. The morning after one of the big TV award shows, people all over the country are discussing it at the water cooler. It's an experience they shared. It's something that connects them.

Organizations seeking to become more aligned are in effect seeking to get everyone feeling more connected. Replacing different and conflicting business priorities with a single overarching objective that everyone can relate to and believe in—this is an exercise in creating a sense of human connection. Orchestrating opportunities for everyone in the organization to be together as part of a single large audience, to be cheering and applauding together (and even cackling with laughter together), is a powerful way to forge deep connections. This is what flashpoint businesses do with the kinds of large-scale award ceremonies described at the start of the chapter. As mentioned a number of times already, there is satisfaction for the applauders as well as for those applauded. The greater the number of applauders, the more satisfying it becomes for all of them to be sharing the experience—and the more motivational it becomes for everyone involved. It creates one of those magical you-had-to-be-there moments.

Many businesses already have periodic all-employee meetings or events that allow for this kind of larger-scale celebration on a fairly regular basis. For those that do not, however, is there an event that can be introduced into the organizational calendar, and that can serve as an ideal forum for such collective celebration?

An especially appropriate event of this type is the "funding-application review meetings" described in Chapter 5. These, you'll recall, are meetings in which employees who have brainstormed ideas for delighting customers—and who are now seeking funding for the implementation of their ideas—formally "make the case" for their project. With the entire employee population in attendance at such meetings, those making applications feel a strong incentive to "play to the audience"—that is, to win over their peers (through humorous skits or irresistible argument, for example) in order to sway management's decision in their favor. This kind of high-energy "fun" event, full of vocal audience reaction, is the perfect setting for two kinds of powerful recognition.

1. Project implementers who have previously secured funding for their own initiatives use the positive customer feedback they've collected to report on their successes. Their fun challenge is to find creative ways to report their results, in order to entertain and impress the audience.
2. Management relates hero stories the honorees themselves may not even know about, based on feedback the *managers* have harvested from delighted customers. Again, the objective is to solicit enthusiastic reactions from the audience.

Such meetings are particularly effective promoters of cultural alignment, because all four steps of the culture-change process are made visible at the same time. The audience hears about how some employees came up with their own ideas for delighting customers (Step One); how management helped make the implementation of those ideas successful (Step Two); and how customers were encouraged to provide positive feedback (Step Three). And now, in the meeting itself, they see firsthand how not only implementers, but *all* employees who went the extra mile for customers, are being hailed as heroes and champions by the entire organization (Step Four).

Such meetings are also particularly motivational forms of recognition, because all four attributes are present. Effort quotient: this all-employee meeting is obviously costly and time-consuming to organize. Internal/external meld: the meeting is organized by management, yet it's customer feedback that's triggering all the applause. Hero story: management describes cases in which employees did things to help brighten customers' lives in some meaningful way. Big audience: the whole employee population gets to participate in the applause, recognition, emotion.

CVS/pharmacy has its Paragon awards, DNC has its Legacy of Service awards—what these (along with every TV award show in existence) make clear is that honorees *treasure* an actual trophy, or plaque, or pin, or other tangible symbol of their achievement they can display with pride long after the fact. Management can therefore enhance the motivational value of the recognition they bestow in these all-employee meetings by creating "best feedback of the week" awards, or special monthly customer-focus awards, or a quarterly "award of excellence," or an annual "President's Award," or any similar award or commemorative prize. Such symbols of achievement are the ultimate time-release motivators; they have the power to continue refueling the winners' motivational engine even *years* after the original third-ring project was first introduced.

The Celebration Life-Cycle of One Success

In Chapter 3 I gave an example of manager Chris trying the four-step culture-change experiment by getting a group of employees to brainstorm ideas for delighting customers. In that example, worker Terry came up with an idea to provide a bench for senior citizens to use while waiting in line.

Now we can observe the various ways by which Terry (and Terry's peers as well) might derive a motivational boost from this one implemented idea over a considerable span of time.

Spontaneous customer feedback. As part of being granted funding for the bench, Terry had to make a commitment to validate the assumption that such a bench would add value for elderly customers. This means Terry had to solicit feedback directly from bench users. The more positive this immediate feedback is, the more motivational its effect on Terry.

Peer-group feedback. Terry is also required to "report back" a summary of the collected customer feedback. This is to take place at next month's "funding-application review meeting," where all the employees will hear about—and react to—Terry's success. Others who have also heard positive feedback about the bench may be invited to share their comments.

Newsletter feature. The following month, the company newsletter runs a story about how the bench came into being. The story includes comments from delighted customers, and a photo of Terry beside the bench. Copies of the newsletter are mailed to members of Terry's family.

Management feedback. Once it's been confirmed that the bench is a hit, Terry's official obligation to collect feedback about it is over. But management incorporates a question about the bench in its customer surveys, or its mystery shopping checklist, or any other measurement mechanisms, in order to continue to receive comments about how deeply the bench is appreciated by some of its users. Samples from this "second wave" of positive feedback are unveiled by management to the entire staff at the next funding-application review meeting—and if warranted by the continuing flow of feedback, at subsequent meetings as well. (Perhaps an especially appreciative customer is invited to attend in person, or to supply comments on a video that is screened at the event.) Terry is invited to stand and take a bow during every event at which the bench is formally cited as a major source of customer delight.

Annual Service Awards. Terry is one of several winners honored at the company's big splashy annual service awards ceremony. Members of Terry's family are invited to attend at the company's expense.

Service Awards coverage in the newsletter. It's customary for the newsletter that immediately follows the annual service awards to devote much of its space to coverage of the event. A photo of Terry holding the award, flanked by family members and top management, is prominently featured.

The cycle of celebration need not end there. As a Service Award winner, Terry may be assigned a special parking spot in the company parking lot, or become eligible for other perks. Terry may be invited to participate in selecting which new ideas from other employees should be granted funding. If the company operates in multiple locations, it may invite Terry to travel at company expense to oversee the installation of similar benches at these other sites.

The above relates to a single implemented idea. Now multiply this by the number of other ideas implemented at the same time as Terry's, and that similarly generate an outpouring of positive customer feedback. And multiply it again by the number of winning ideas that emerge from *future* rounds of employee brainstorming and are celebrated at future funding-application review meetings.

A flashpoint culture is a culture of celebration. These businesses virtually *always* have something to celebrate. And fundamental to all of it is the fact that it's an externally-derived measure of customer satisfaction that's being celebrated, not an internally-derived measure of profit or some other index of organizational self-interest. Celebrations of this kind awaken the "spirit of volunteerism" that may be lying dormant within many employees—their basic human need to feel useful and necessary in the world. Even as they applaud their fellow employees, they privately aspire to have their turn as the ones being hailed for accomplishing such worthwhile things. Each celebration of success intensifies the aspirational field. One by one the iron filings come into alignment.

Frequent celebration of successes is one of the key things management does to mirror the effort employees are making to delight customers. *One* of the key things—but not the *only* thing.

Employees will often discover that despite their best efforts to delight customers, there remain certain cultural roadblocks that still get in the way.

The elimination of roadblocks is how we sustain our collective motivational momentum over the longer term. That's next.

Notes

1. Pamela Miller, Blue Cross Blue Shield of New Jersey, interview with the author for Paul Levesque, *Breakaway Planning: 8 Big Questions to Guide Organizational Change* (Amacom, 1998).
2. Eileen Howard Dunn, CVS/pharmacy, interview with the author for Paul Levesque, *Customer Service Made Easy* (Entrepreneur Press, 2006).
3. Stewart Collins, DNC, interview with the author, October 31, 2006.
4. Wayne S. Charness, Hasbro, interview with the author for Paul Levesque, *Customer Service Made Easy* (Entrepreneur Press, 2006).
5. Stewart Collins interview.
6. Cheryl Beall, Retail 101, interview with the author, October 20, 2006.

7. Ibid.
8. Brian Gallagher, Lindt & Sprüngli, interview with the author, November 15, 2006.
9. Stewart Collins interview.
10. Brian Gallagher interview.
11. Stewart Collins interview.
12. Camille Maxwell, DNC, interview ith the author, October 31, 2006.
13. Ibid.
14. Mark Emmitte, Stage Stores, interview with the author, December 5, 2006.
15. Beth Guastella, Kate Spade, interview with the author, November 10, 2006.
16. Stewart Collins interview.
17. Beth Guastella interview.

Keeping the Motivational Kettle Boiling

Chapter 8

The premise behind many word-association games is that over time some words become almost inseparably linked to others. Few people ever speak of "canine beings" or "feline beings," for example, whereas the expression "human beings" is extremely common. And something many human beings may not like is that the word *disgruntled* is linked to the word *employees* often enough to similarly turn the two into a familiar everyday expression. "Disgruntled" is defined in the Webster's dictionary on my bookshelf as meaning ill-humored or discontented. Yet even that same dictionary makes an immediate link to employees, when it provides a single example for correct usage of the word: "The workers are disgruntled with their wages."[1]

Now of course we can't expect dictionary lexicographers to also be experts in organizational dynamics. That dictionary example of proper usage may be *linguistically* correct—but we know that when it comes to the true sources of employee disgruntlement, "wages" are seldom at the top of the list. And even when the list seems to go on and on ("We aren't given any say in how things are done around here," "Our priorities are always being changed," "Those clowns in the _____ department are making things impossible for us"), all of these are typically *symptoms* of a single cultural ailment: lack of alignment.

This book began with a discussion of cultural "chilling factors" that undermine most management attempts to raise the motivational temperature within organizations. Chapter 2 was devoted to the biggest demotivator of them all—a predominant cultural focus on self-interest, the number-one cause of employee cynicism. But though this may be the *biggest* employee demotivator, it's seldom the *only* one. We turn our attention now to some of those second-tier demotivators that have helped make "disgruntled employees" such a familiar phrase.

Interference Patterns

Chapter 3 made reference to an "aspirational field" that can pull random cultural elements into alignment, the way a magnetic field can affect random iron filings on a sheet of paper. Naturally, if in addition to the primary magnet there are individual smaller magnets in the vicinity of the filings, each positioned at a different angle, this will make it more difficult to discern a single clear axis of magnetic alignment. Multiple fields will create interference. If enough are present, they may cancel out the effect of the primary field altogether.

Our four-step process for culture change has a proven ability to create a powerful aspirational field. But there may be other existing influences, embedded deeply in the culture, that interfere with this dominant field. They may have the power to weaken it over time. In combination, they may even have the power to cancel it out altogether.

To maintain the motivational momentum created by the four-step process, it will first be essential to discover where secondary sources of misalignment may be hiding within the culture. (Some of the most likely hiding places are enumerated below.) It's then a matter of bringing them into alignment with the primary field, each in their turn.

Taken in isolation, every one of the countless operational systems, policies, procedures, and processes that collectively define "the way we do things around here" could potentially be a source of interference. It would of course be impossible to scrutinize all of these—and correct every one that needs to be brought into alignment—overnight. The more effective approach would be to attack the most influential culprits first, and gradually work our way down the list.

We can broadly distinguish between two types of operational demotivators: those whose negative effect is felt most directly on the customer side of things at first (which we'll call "customer side") and those that more directly and immediately affect *employees* ("employee side").

Examples of customer-side demotivators might include return-and-refund policies, the organization's hours of operation, a cumbersome and inefficient automated phone system, paperwork that's unclear or tedious to fill out, long waits caused by understaffing or process bottlenecks, an undersized or poorly-lit parking area, and so on. The list could be a long one—but what every item on the list has in common is that it represents *an obstacle to customer delight over which the employees have no control.* No matter how diligently the workers endeavor to expand customers' perceptions of value into the third ring, these roadblocks to delight keep shrinking perceptions back toward the inner or second rings.

This is why these customer-side obstacles quickly turn into mirror-image *employee* demotivators. As workers' efforts to deliver delight are undermined by factors they cannot control, enthusiasm turns into frustration and resentment. Businesses suffering from the Big Disconnect invariably assume their employees can't deliver delight because they're demotivated. (The only "remedy" they know is to continue trying to "fix the employees" through incentives, prizes, etc.) Businesses that begin to see things more clearly soon recognize it's more often the other way around: employees are demotivated because they can't deliver delight. An altogether different malady, calling for an altogether different remedy—one that involves "fixing the culture." As Beth Guastella sums it up, "The way that an employee feels, and their happiness, and their job satisfaction—the way they feel when they come in every day—has everything to do with how they interact and react with the customer. Without question."[2]

Consistent with creating a culture of greater employee involvement and ownership, the most effective way to identify and remove customer-side operational obstacles is to get the *employees* doing it. In our process for culture change, employees (while brainstorming ways to improve the overall customer experience) almost invariably pinpoint the biggest existing roadblocks to customer delight.

It's a logical extension of their brainstorming activity to get them coming up with their own ideas for how to eliminate the problem. If there are costs or changes in management policy associated with whatever solution(s) they have in mind, they can "make the case" for their solution as part of a regular funding-application review meeting. If a successful implementation of their solution produces a new source of positive customer feedback, the organization has transformed a motivational chilling factor into a heating factor. And in the case of obstacles that (for regulatory or other reasons) simply cannot be removed—at least these obstacles should no longer be a source of employee resentment. If workers are allowed to try to find a way around some such obstacle, and discover for themselves there simply *is* no way around it, they can no longer blame it on their "uncaring" management team. It predisposes them to do all they can to minimize the obstacle's negative impact on customers.

Employee-side demotivators constitute a different category. These typically relate to such purely internal issues as how job promotions are posted and handled; how new employees are selected; sick-leave, time off, overtime, and vacation policies; the performance evaluation process; and so on. In some cases the list here, too, could be a long one. No matter how great the workers' initial enthusiasm for taking care of customers, their concern quickly turns to taking care of *themselves* in a work setting that seems determined to shortchange them the moment they let down their guard. This is why employee-side demotivators quickly also turn into mirror-image *customer* problems. As workers' attention shifts to self-interest, customers find themselves encountering varying degrees of neglect and indifference.

Employee-side demotivators don't logically belong in the kinds of employee brainstorming sessions described above. In those, it's workers looking for creative ways to eliminate obstacles to customer delight. This time, it's managers who must become creative and find ways to eliminate obstacles to *employee* delight.

Two frequent sources of cultural misalignment are the organization's hiring process, and its performance evaluation process. We can use these two examples to illustrate how the interference factor can be reduced, if not eliminated, in other internal systems and processes as well.

Reinforcing Alignment Through the Hiring Process

New people coming into any business can bring with them new ideas, new experience, new energy. Their presence can strengthen the existing culture—but it can also weaken it. Sometimes a huge influx of new people can take place virtually overnight, such as through mergers and acquisitions. In this kind of sudden upheaval, two entirely different organizational cultures often end up being cobbled together into a mish-mash that ends up looking unfamiliar—and unappealing—to everyone involved. New people can also arrive one individual at a time, through the hiring process. If these new people are collectively diluting or weakening the organizational culture, the danger is that the change is so gradual it can go unnoticed.

A differentiating characteristic of flashpoint businesses in general is that they recognize the value and importance of the culture they have created, and they consciously take steps to safeguard it. In more conventional businesses, the question of "culture" virtually never enters into management discussions, or even into management thinking. If there are job positions to be filled in a conventional business, the only thing everyone seems to consider important is finding candidates with the right experience and academic qualifications. In flashpoint businesses, by comparison, *passion* and a "values fit" take precedence.

"The most challenging issue around hiring practices," says Novations Group's Peter Ambrozaitis, "is hiring to the passion of an individual to be in alignment with what the organizational needs are." He cites his firm's trademarked "TOP" model: "We create career bests within individuals when we align an associate's Talents and Passion with organizational needs."[3]

"The biggest thing I look for, especially nowadays," says Brian Gallagher at Lindt & Sprüngli, "is a personality fit culturally within the organization.... It's, 'How will you fit in personality-wise with the overall culture of this group or this organization?' It's the single biggest thing I look for."

What tells Brian he may have found a good candidate? "For the most part—and this may just come from having been hiring people for the better part of 15 years—it's being able to walk away and not question whether somebody was being up-front or not.... I have a rule, that if you tell me something that I've heard from somebody else, you now have to give me at least one—if not two—levels of either explanation or live examples.... And that's really where the gut instinct takes you to, okay, they didn't have to hesitate, they were able to give me this and were able to understand what the outcome was. When they can't do that, you sort of [wonder] if it was the rote answer that they read in a book somewhere, maybe written by one Paul Levesque, or if it was something that they truly believe in."[4]

"You can teach skills," says retail consultant Cheryl Beall, "you can teach anyone to do something better, but you cannot teach people to be nice, and you cannot teach them to have good judgment. I just truly believe that.... Most of the time, bad hiring decisions happen because people are desperate to get a body.... The manager that doesn't have somebody in that spot for a very long time, all of sudden these candidates start looking better and better. And so, at the root of it, what needs to happen is ... keep an eye out for good service, and people that are engaging and seem to enjoy being around other people, people that have good socialization skills.

I find that culturally, people have less and less ability to socialize just on a polite level and know how to just have a nice conversation with someone and chat about things other than themselves." I remind Cheryl of the old joke about the self-absorbed actor who says, "But hey, enough about me, let's talk about you for a while—what do *you* think of me?" "Precisely," Cheryl says. "If people could for five minutes quit thinking about themselves—find people like that and put them in your business. You can teach them how to do the math.... And people are not looking for employees until they have a vacancy, and I think that's a real problem, and so you wind up hiring out of desperation, and the result is pretty darn obvious."[5]

"One of the things we talk about when we work with clients," says Novations Group's Cathi Rittelmann, "is the tendency we have to hire in our own image, and then be disappointed with the results."

Cathi describes a sign she spotted on the wall of one of the big coffee chains: "[The sign said] 'If you love our coffee, you'd love working for us.' To be able to tap into that passion that people have for the product ... I think is an ingenious way to look for employees." She describes a common mistake made by those who conduct job interviews. "Part of an interview process typically is, 'Let me describe our culture for you, and you tell me how you think you could fit into this.'" As she suggests, this approach makes it far too easy for candidates to supply answers of the rote "telling-'em-only-what-they-want-to-hear" type Brian Gallagher decries above. Far better, says Cathi, is to ask "'What kind of a culture are you looking for, and what would make you happiest?' The message is, 'You need to prove that you belong here.'"[6]

Hiring for a cultural fit is one of the important ways managers protect the motivational culture they have worked hard to create. Pessimistic or cynical individuals are "screened out"—even despite otherwise impressive qualifications—to avoid introducing elements of nonalignment into the work setting. This kind of hiring is not difficult; in fact, in many ways it *simplifies* the whole selection process. When more than one candidate with the appropriate experience or qualifications applies for a given position, the final decision will often be made on a flip-of-the-coin basis. When passion and other aspects of cultural compatibility become the principal selection criteria, however, one of the otherwise similar candidates almost always stands out from the rest. The only reason so few businesses hire for cultural fit is because they have not yet learned to *see* the value of doing so. Just one more grim side effect of that particular form of blindness we've been referring to as the big disconnect.

Related to the hiring process is the orientation session for new hires, an especially effective way to "imprint" the culture of the organization on new people from day one. A great many businesses miss a glorious opportunity to reinforce alignment in their employee orientation sessions. Their inclination is to tell of the company's history—a great historical saga that's focused on the past and *concludes* with the present day. The newcomer may get the impression he or she has joined the outfit just a bit too late, with all of its glory days behind it. A better imprint is one that conveys that the real glory days lie just ahead, and the newcomer has arrived just in the nick of time to be part of an exciting future. The orientation is a success if on the evening of the newcomer's first day, at the dinner table, loved ones hear about his or her amazing good fortune to have joined a winning team just before they begin accomplishing truly exciting things—things he or she will be actively involved in bringing about.

Reinforcing Alignment Through Performance Evaluations

THE RAISE

ACT I, SCENE II

Roger and Helen are seated at the breakfast table.

The mood is sullen and quiet, after the previous night's quarrel about finances.

ROGER: Look, honey, I know our credit cards have been getting out of hand. But next month is my performance review.

HELEN (without looking up from her cereal): Performance review?

ROGER: At work. That's where I find out what kind of raise I'll be getting.

HELEN (looking at him): Really? They're going to be giving you a raise?

ROGER: Honey, that's what performance reviews are *for*. After all the extra work I did over the summer on the overseas project, this time they're *bound* to give me a good one.

HELEN (returning to her cereal): Well, they'd better.

Like millions of others, Roger has what he considers a clear understanding of what performance reviews are for.

"Performance management systems" says Cathi Rittelmann, "have traditionally attached performance appraisals to monetary increases." As with our discussion in the previous chapter around the hazards of tying financial reward to recognition, Cathi believes linking monetary issues into the performance evaluation process is counterproductive in exactly the same way. "People finally say, 'Okay, fine, if I'm not going to get that level of satisfaction [from my job], I'm going to squeeze as much money out of it and get as much sort of pseudo-recognition as I can—be it [a new] title, be it vacation days, whatever. So because we tie our perception of someone's performance to what they should be paid, it all becomes worth the same to me as an employee. Companies now are choosing to separate the two more overtly, to say performance management or performance appraisals will be totally separate from increases."[7]

If Roger is wrong, if the ideal function of performance evaluations is *not* to provide a salary adjustment (along with all the demotivational reasons why the adjustment isn't any bigger), then what exactly *is* its function?

Throughout much of this book I've used DNC's *GuestPath* program as a model example of a culture-shaping initiative that promotes alignment on a multitude of levels. It's worth recalling that the starting point for the entire program was the creation of a set of basic *performance standards*. In Chapter 4 Stewart Collins itemizes how "... We have our Universal Service Standards, we have our Operating Standards, we have a Continuous Improvement Cycle that we do with the standards, [we deliver] training to the standards, [we focus on] measuring, rewarding, closing the gap." He also stresses that the actual standards themselves were "organically grown"—that is, in an example of employee involvement and ownership, the standards were arrived at by people within the company. "That organic process of going through the pain of figuring out what those 10 'universals' were going to be was so powerful—even though those 10 are so simple," he says.[8]

The power of this approach is felt in two ways. First, because the standards are defined by the kinds of employees whose performance is going to be measured against them, there's no backlash of resentment toward management. No one can complain that these standards are unrealistic, or unfair, or are being imposed on unwilling employees. Second, the simple *existence* of clearly defined performance standards gives performance evaluations a completely different—and far more productive—reason for being.

Where job priorities keep shifting and changing, where workers are never quite sure what it is that's actually expected of them, formal evaluations of their performance become a meaningless exercise. Many underperforming employees know full well it's management's own lack of clear standards that's largely to blame; negative evaluations of their performance, especially with a punitive element attached, become a major source of resentment, cynicism, and demotivation.

"You want to talk about how you keep people motivated?" says Brian Gallagher. "You don't blind-side them. If I have to have a hard conversation with somebody about a policy that they didn't follow, that's a very different conversation if they *could've* followed it and they just didn't, as opposed to, is it an argument because there *was* no defined policy, and [if so, then] why am I coming down on them now? You can't go from situation to situation applying what is perceived as a different set of rules [each time], and that's the thing that happens when you don't have a defined policy and procedure. And I link those two. You should not, in my mind, have policy without procedure. If all I have is policy that says, 'In this situation do this,' then I can no longer come and talk to one store who did it one way about why that's not good because another store did it another way which was better. If I can clearly define, 'Here's what our policy is, so here's our expectation, and here's how we expect you to perform that,' there is no gray area. And the more gray area that can be eliminated, the more it can be a business-advancing discussion as opposed to an opinionated discussion. And that's huge."[9]

"It's very important to communicate to the employees what the expectations are," Cheryl Beall agrees, "and I'm not sure that that's always done well. I think that it's probably better to have shorter and more frequent performance evaluations that are very specific to a few key points that will directly impact the customer and the business. Most managers that I encounter are like, 'Oh my god, we're doing reviews or we're doing mid-years,' and they're so over it by the time they're doing it that the quality of it is bad, and by the time they sit down with the employee they can't give them the time that's necessary."[10]

"People perform to the things that they're going to be measured to," says Peter Ambrozaitis. "So when organizations come to us and they say that 'We want to have better selling behaviors on the sales floor,' or 'We want our managers to be more effective leaders,' one of the first questions I ask is, "How are you currently measuring that on their performance evaluations?' And it's astounding when organizations say, 'Well, we don't really have that included on their performance evaluation process.'"[11]

A performance evaluation is not successful, Brian Gallagher believes, "… unless it concludes with a path for future improvement—and that goes for somebody who scores well or somebody who scores poorly."[12]

"For me," says Beth Guastella, "the review process, it's not about telling them what they've done wrong, [nor] just what they've done right. It's a developmental tool used to certainly celebrate the success of the past year, but most importantly, to map out the coming year. What is the path that this individual or professional is going to follow in order to grow? … Not just what is your goal for them, but what are *their* goals, what is it they want out of their job? And then helping them to achieve that, as well as making sure it [also] mirrors the objectives of the company."[13]

Our Chapter 1 exploration of making work feel like play touched on a key element that makes play activities fun: "a clear set of rules, understood by all." The players understand what the objective of the game is, and what the rules do—and don't—allow them to do to achieve it. The rules are simple, straightforward, and easy to remember. These rules are *performance standards*, plain and simple. They make play activities more satisfying, and they also make work activities more satisfying. If a business can accept the idea that productivity improves when workers derive enjoyment from the work they do, it will also see the value in working with employees to create clear performance standards for every job. Once such standards are in place, performance evaluations become one more "time-release motivator"—another opportunity to celebrate successes and intensify alignment.

The above gives examples of how the hiring process and the performance evaluation process can be put into the service of cultural alignment over the long term. A similar approach can be applied to all the various operational systems and policies and processes and procedures within any business enterprise. In most cases doing so does not entail a radical overhaul of all the operational elements involved. It often requires no more than a minor adjustment, just enough to let employees easily see for themselves how this or that piece, too, has a clear and direct link to the one single overarching objective that drives the organization from top to bottom, across the board. All employees at all levels must be able to see—at all times—how every arrow in the place is pointing in the same direction.

"You know all the conversations, the cartoons you see about 'What's The Meaning Of Life,'" says Cathi Rittelmann. "And I always think it's such a simple answer—and [this is a] question [that] translates itself to everything, whether it's our job, or what we're doing today in the house, or whatever. It really means, 'What the heck am I supposed to be doing?'.... The meaning of life really isn't [one] big answer, it's just *an* answer. So give me an answer about where I should be headed, boss. *An* answer. So tell me what the answer is, and where I need to go.... Until you give me the answer, I can't figure out what questions I need to ask myself to get there. Motivation is such an emotional touch point.... All you have to do is be able to give people the outcome. 'Here's where we need to end up.... Okay, roll up our sleeves, and together we'll figure out a way to get there.' And brainstorm, and give [people] the latitude to try new things. How cool is that?"[14]

"It's very contagious," Cheryl Beall declares. What does she believe is so contagious? "It's the enthusiasm. Enthusiasm, and a greater belief that things *can* change, you know, that [employees] *can* have an impact on something."[15]

The four-step culture-change process is how the flashpoint effect's contagious enthusiasm gets started. The gradual fine-tuning of every operational element, to bring all of them each in turn into alignment, is how the flashpoint effect is maintained over the longer term.

In Praise of Realistic Expectations

Archie Felskie is confident he can live forever. "The second hundred years will be the real test," he says.

Just how foolproof is the culture-change process outlined in this book? Alas, nothing in this imperfect world is *completely* foolproof, despite extravagant advertising claims to the contrary. Give enough fools enough time, and they'll eventually find a way to bring down just about anything, as we were all very painfully reminded not so many years ago.

Businesses in perfect alignment do not become magically invulnerable to global economic or political upheavals over which they have no control. Even flashpoint businesses make mistakes—sometimes serious ones. Even highly motivated workers have bad days. And there are some employees in this world who have no intention of *ever* getting on board. There are some customers who have no intention of *ever* experiencing delight—and who, even if they do, certainly have no intention of ever admitting it out loud.

There is also, however, the following to take into account.

While no businesses are immune to the larger economic or political forces around them, businesses with strong alignment always withstand these better than the rest. Although flashpoint businesses can still make mistakes, thanks to greater employee and customer loyalty they can also recover from these more easily. Energized workers are not exempted from bad days—but it happens far less often to them than to most. It's true that there'll always be some workers and some customers who have no intention of ever playing ball—but the flashpoint effect has the power to *change* intentions, at least in some cases.

In terms of cultivating realistic expectations, one of the good-news aspects of the process described in these pages is that "total failure" would represent a situation in which things simply didn't get any better. That's really about the worst that can happen. This approach to motivation may not be foolproof, but it is highly fool-*resistant*. For the process to do any real damage, someone would need to make a great and deliberate effort to sabotage it. And even then—a process designed to generate *delight* on all sides would represent an extremely poor choice of weapon with which to try and crush the spirit of an organization.

Another expectation worth cultivating relates what we might call the "forgiveness factor." If we've learned to see how employee motivation and customer satisfaction are always mirror-images of each other, then we're also equipped to see how the forgiveness factor works on both sides of the hidden mirror.

We already know what we call "customer loyalty" has a built-in forgiveness factor: loyal customers will be more disposed to forgive a mistake or a lapse made by a business that's visibly committed to their delight. The mirror image of this kind of forgiveness also applies: loyal employees are more disposed to forgive a mistake or a lapse made by an employer that's visibly committed to their delight. Where there's alignment toward a single objective everyone cares about—where that basic need for a motive is being met—there's a greater willingness to make do with less-than-perfect chairs, or less-than-ideal lighting, or less than extravagant wages.

As part of implementing this process for culture change, honest mistakes may well be made. But the more workers can see an effort to provide them with a satisfying sense of purpose in their jobs, the more we can expect them to be forgiving when they encounter other shortcomings in their workplace.

Closing Arguments

Our topic has been "employee motivation"—and it's easy to assume we've been talking only about *frontline* employees.

Most managers expect workers to cite "money" as their primary motivator—yet if you ask these same managers what their *own* primary motivator was when they were starting out, virtually none will cite money. Somehow, as they rise up through the ranks and assume supervisory and then management positions, they come to believe that the workers under their authority are different from themselves in some fundamental way. They come to believe that what matters to these workers are not the same things that used to matter to themselves—and that *still* matter to themselves. But every once in a while a senior manager dares to let down the facade of having risen "above all that," and we get a reminder that everyone in an organization—*everyone*—is really yearning for the same kind of connection to something meaningful in their work lives.

This was brought home to me after I'd concluded my interview with Cathi Rittelmann for this book. We were going through a kind of cheerful wrapping-up procedure, when she grew reflective and shared an off-the-cuff observation. "What's also funny in terms of motivation," she said, "is how sad the people sometimes are when they don't feel motivated, or engaged by their manager. In some individuals there's an intrinsic sadness about the fact that they can't somehow make it work."

This struck a chord with me. Working with client organizations over the years, I've tended to be more aware of the cynicism of disgruntled workers, of their anger and their vocal resistance. Until hearing Cathi put it into words, I hadn't really thought too much about the deeper, quieter, more private sadness that lies below the surface. I encouraged her to continue. She referred to a particular client organization in a particular city where something unexpected had recently taken place—but I'll leave both the client and the city unnamed, to avoid embarrassing anyone. "[Client name] is a company we just started to work with," she told me, "and about a month and half ago I went to—they're based out of [name of city], they're a family-owned company, it was the executive committee that I was working with that day." She explained that as is her custom, she'd asked the group to "... think about the best manager you've ever had, and what [did it] feel like to work for that person, and how engaged were you....

"There was a guy in there who's the CFO, and he popped his hand right up—and [he] hadn't been talking for the first I bet 45 minutes—and he stood up and he said, 'I felt energized. I felt passionate. I felt engaged.' Those were the three words he used: energized, passionate, and engaged. I said, 'Why? What did that person do?' And so he described it. And [then] he said, 'You know, I don't any more.' Which was a hell of a bombshell to drop. He said, "I'm sad about it. I'm sad that I can't seem to get my foothold here. I can't seem to figure out what it is I'm supposed to contribute toward.'" Cathi paused for a moment. "It became a whole different executive session," she said. "But how [moving] is it to watch somebody who's a professional, [with] experience at that level, who is saddened to not be able to find a foothold to be engaged or motivated ...."[16]

This brings some related personal memories to mind. I have many times found myself sitting in on routine executive-level meetings in which there was no laughter, no pleasure in the room whatsoever. Over the years I've heard my share of grim tales about ruthless "office politics." I've listened to managers describe how they felt betrayed by other managers, and managers who believed they'd been in line for a juicy promotion and were devastated when they were passed over. I've heard gossip about this manager's secret drinking problem and that manager's secret marital woes. I've watched managers sweat through presentations reporting dismal financial results, and presentations that announced layoffs and closures.

A memory of one particularly troubling kind sticks with me. It's something I've witnessed often, in many different organizational settings. It happens in the boardroom, usually, during senior management meetings. Someone in the meeting cracks a joke of some kind, related to some aspect of the business. The exact split second the remark is made, all eyes in the room turn in perfect unison to the CEO. That's a sight I find disturbing. Someone makes a funny wisecrack, and a whole group of well-educated, nicely dressed, grown-up professionals immediately look to their leader *to see if it's okay to laugh*. What kind of sadness does insecurity at that level instill in a person? When managers are feeling as paralyzed and fearful as this, how likely are they to care about some process for cheering up their frontline workers?

Those frontline workers enjoy wisecracks too. Sometimes they *display* their wisecracks in their workspaces or on their vehicles.

It's not hard to find examples like the above. They're everywhere. Workers photocopy items like these and distribute them around the workplace. They e-mail them to friends all over the world. These little jokes make us smile. But now take another, closer look. If you concentrate hard enough, they become like optical illusions—the meaning of the image "flips" before your eyes, from funny to sad. Every one of these clever little slogans and catchy punch lines is a declaration of despair. For those workers who identify deeply enough with these sentiments to display them as manifestos, how does their underlying sadness color their personal relationships, their conversations at the dinner table, the last thoughts that occupy their minds as they lie awake in the darkness at night? How often do they, too, find themselves lost in a silent lonely struggle to try and "figure out what it is I'm supposed to contribute toward"? If we want to play armchair-sociologist for just a moment, what connection (if any) might there be between despair in the workplace and broader social ills like alcohol abuse, depression, domestic violence, and divorce?

I can only speculate about that. What I do know for sure, though, is every time I encounter a management team bemoaning how difficult it is to keep employees motivated, it means I'm dealing with another organization that does not yet understand how to provide the kind of basic motive all workers crave. Any time I hear managers grumbling about their demotivated workers, I'm always tempted to ask, "Tell me, just confidentially, do you suppose they're demotivated 24 hours a day—or just the eight hours a day they spend with you?"

As I write these words, I'm well aware the majority of businesses operating today do not make work feel like play. They do not define a single overarching objective that is outwardly focused. They do not maximize employee involvement and ownership in efforts to improve the customer experience. They do not set out to make their workers look like heroes in customers' eyes. They do not take time every day to celebrate successes and hero stories. Their workers show up because they need to, not because they want to—and that's if they show up at all. For management-level personnel in virtually all organizations, there's one basic motivator: positive business results being driven by their own enthusiastic teams of workers. When that basic motivator is absent, even people in management positions find it hard to drag themselves to work every day. They find themselves updating their resumes at their desks when no one's looking. Down the corridor, in the break room, their workers are scanning the newspaper job listings when no one's looking.

We often hear inspiring words about the entrepreneurial spirit, the spirit of innovation, the American spirit. It's less uplifting to be reminded that millions of our workers are in fact utterly dispirited. It's not because the kind of work they do tends by its very nature to crush their spirit. In every line of work that exists, in every industry, you can find organizations where the collective spirit of the workforce has been completely extinguished, and others where employees are burning bright with energy and enthusiasm. Failure to provide workers with a compelling motive to enjoy their work is ultimately, finally, and always, a failure of leadership.

We can only hope future generations won't look back on our failings too harshly.

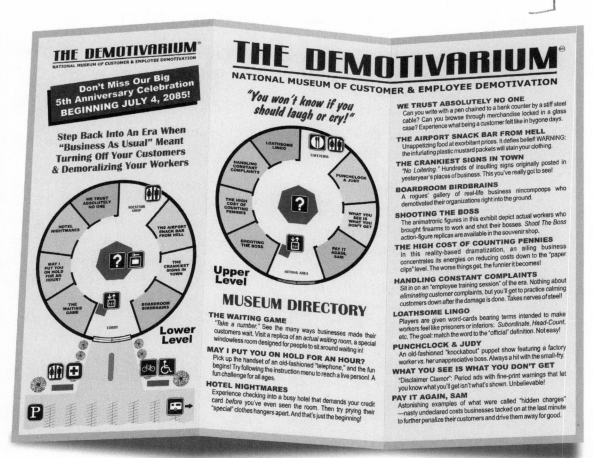

Let's not let it come to this.

Notes

1. *Webster's Ninth New Collegiate Dictionary* (Markham, Ontario: Thomas Allen & Son Ltd., 1983).
2. Beth Guastella, Kate Spade, interview with the author, November 10, 2006.
3. Peter Ambrozaitis, Novations Group, interview with the author, December 28, 2006.
4. Brian Gallagher, Lindt & Sprüngli, interview with the author, November 15, 2006.
5. Cheryl Beall, Retail 101, interview with the author, October 20, 2006.
6. Cathi Rittelmann, Novations Group, interview with the author, January 16, 2007.
7. Ibid.
8. Stewart Collins, DNC, interview with the author, October 31, 2006.
9. Brian Gallagher interview.
10. Cheryl Beall interview.
11. Peter Ambrozaitis interview.
12. Brian Gallagher interview.
13. Beth Guastella interview.
14. Cathi Rittelmann interview.
15. Cheryl Beall interview.
16. Cathi Rittelmann interview.

Index

About the Author

Paul Levesque is an author, seminar leader, and public speaker with over two decades' experience as an international customer focus consultant. For ten years he served as an executive consultant with the Achieve Group, and was lead instructor at Achieve's *Service Quality Academy*. He's an associate of Boston-based Novations Group Inc., and is also founder and CEO of Customer Focus Breakthroughs Inc.

Paul delivers keynote speeches and management workshops across North America and around the world. He has spoken to business leaders from Morocco to the Baltic Sea, across Europe and Australia, and in most major American and Canadian cities. His previous books include *Breakaway Planning: 8 Big Questions To Guide Organizational Change* (Amacom, 1998), and *Customer Service Made Easy* (Entrepreneur Press, 2006). Paul's articles have appeared in such publications as *Quality Digest*, Canada's national newspaper *The Globe and Mail*, England's *Personnel Today Management Resources Guidebook*, and on the *Entrepreneur.com* and *MSNBC.com* websites.

This is Paul's fifth book. To learn more about building a highly-motivated "flashpoint culture" in your business, visit **www.customerfocusbreakthroughs.com**.